# Master Atlas

**Other books by Edward MacNeal**

*Mathsemantics: Making Numbers Talk Sense* (New York: Viking, 1994)

*The Semantics of Air Passenger Transportation* (Norfolk [Va.] Port and Industrial Authority, 1981)

# MacNeal's
# Master Atlas of Decision Making

*A new kind of guide to the maps
people use in making up their minds*

Edward MacNeal

*with*
Commentary by Russell Joyner
Art by Vince Benedict and Elaine Vogt

INTERNATIONAL SOCIETY FOR GENERAL SEMANTICS
CONCORD, CALIFORNIA

MACNEAL'S MASTER ATLAS OF DECISION MAKING:
A NEW KIND OF GUIDE TO THE MAPS PEOPLE USE
IN MAKING UP THEIR MINDS

Copyright © 1997 by Edward MacNeal. All rights reserved.

Published originally in ten installments in *Et cetera: A Review of General Semantics*, vol. 44, no. 3 through vol. 46, no. 4 (Fall 1987-Winter 1989). Copyright Edward MacNeal.

Grateful acknowledgment is made for permission to reprint the editor's forewords from *Et cetera: A Review of General Semantics*, copyright 1987, 1988, 1989 by the International Society for General Semantics.

Printed in the United States of America

International Society for General Semantics
P.O. Box 728
Concord, CA 94522, USA

**Library of Congress Cataloging-in-Publication Data**

MacNeal, Edward, 1925-
 [Master atlas of decision making]
 MacNeal's master atlas of decision making : a new kind of guide to the maps people use in making up their minds / Edward MacNeal ; with commentary by Russell Joyner ; art by Vince Benedict and Elaine Vogt.
       p.     cm.
  "Published originally in ten installments in Et cetera: a review of general semantics, vol. 44, no. 3 through vol. 46, no. 4 (fall 1987-winter 1989)" —T.p. verso.
  Includes bibliographical references and index.
  ISBN 0-918970-44-X
  1. Decision- making.  2. General semantics.  I. Joyner, Russell, 1924-1996.  II. Title.
  BF448.M33   1997
  153. 8'3—dc21                                                                  97-2441
                                                                                        CIP

To Priscilla

# Contents

|  |  |
|---|---|
| List of tables | ix |
| List of maps | x |
| Acknowledgments | xi |
| Introduction | xii |

1. **Groundwork**
   - *Commentary one* — 1
   - Maps and territories — 4
   - Decisions and maps — 7
   - Three hazards — 10

2. **More groundwork**
   - *Commentary two* — 13
   - The big picture — 15
   - Subdecisional events—situations & alternaquences — 18

3. **Logics for the single decision**
   - *Commentary three* — 25
   - The two simplest patterns (absolute & action-comparative) — 27
   - The commonest pattern (responsive) — 29
   - The most touted pattern (goal-directed) — 33

4. **More logics for the single decision**
   - *Commentary four* — 37
   - The sleeper (originative) — 39
   - The scorecard pattern — 42

5. **Logics for interconnected decisions**
   - *Commentary five* — 47
   - The slippery link (transformative) — 49
   - The vital link (recursive) — 50
   - The unavoidable link (allocative) — 51

6. **More logics for interconnected decisions**
   - *Commentary six* — 61
   - The basic human link (propositional) — 63
   - Two more human links—#1: mutual — 64
   - —#2: reciprocal — 65
   - The extrahuman links (organizational) — 66
   - The web (demasystems) — 72

7. **Applying demalogics**
    *Commentary seven* — 75
    Overview — 77
    A walk through the demagarden — 79
    Error — 81
    Forecasting — 84
    Demaconsciousness — 86

8. **More on applying demalogics**
    *Commentary eight* — 89
    Responsibility — 91
    Verbal clues and levers — 92
    Not just words — 96
    The complete decider — 98
    "Not all" — 99

**Appendices**
    *Commentary nine* — 104
  A. Summary of demalogical structures — 105
  B. Glossary — 112
    *Commentary ten* — 118
  C. At the demalogical helm *(a textual explication)* — 120
  D. Sample demalogical-dictionary entries — 123
  E. Demalogical thesaurus *(abridged)* — 125
  F. Sources — 135

  Index — 137

# Tables

| | | |
|---|---|---|
| 1. | Demalogical masterchart | 16 |
| 2. | Two demaformulas *(absolute and action-comparative)* | 29 |
| 3. | Responsive demaformula | 31 |
| 4. | Goal-directed demaformula | 34 |
| 5. | Sampling of goal-directed words | 36 |
| 6. | Originative demaformula | 40 |
| 7. | Basic demapatterns *(absolute, action-comparative, responsive, goal-directed, and originative)* | 43 |
| 8. | Two scorecard demaformulas | 43 |
| 9. | Transformative demalinkage | 49 |
| 10. | Recursive demalinkage | 50 |
| 11. | Allocative demalinkage | 52 |
| 12. | Basic demalinkages *(transformative, recursive, and allocative)* | 54 |
| 13. | Propositional demalinkage | 64 |
| 14. | Mutual demalinkage | 65 |
| 15. | Reciprocal demalinkage | 66 |
| 16. | Demaspecies comparisons *(person & organization)* | 67 |
| 17. | Organizational demalinkages *(enfounding, enstaffing, functionarial, and second-order)* | 68 |
| 18. | The organizational demalinkage | 68 |
| 19. | Demaunits and functionaries | 69 |
| 20. | Demalogical emphasis | 71 |
| 21. | Demasystems demalinkage | 73 |
| 22. | Errors in a four-demalogic world | 82 |
| 23. | Symptoms of demalogical overreliance | 83 |
| 24. | Demalogically loaded questions | 91 |
| 25. | Some uses of selected demalogics *(absolute, responsive, goal-directed, originative, scorecard, transformative, and allocative)* | 96 |

**Decision-making maps** *(Demamaps)*

| | |
|---|---|
| Subdecisional events *(situation, alternaquence [course of action + consequences])* | 23 |
| Absolute pattern | 27 |
| Action-comparative pattern | 28 |
| Responsive pattern | 30 |
| Forced response *(within responsive pattern)* | 32 |
| Goal-directed pattern | 33 |
| Originative pattern | 39 |
| Scorecard pattern | 44 |
| Mutual linkage | 65 |
| Reciprocal linkage | 66 |
| Compound goal-directed and responsive pattern | 79 |
| Demalogical selection walk | 80 |

# Acknowledgments

My most heartfelt debt is to the late Russell Joyner for taking the initiative. Without him this book wouldn't exist. On learning in 1981 that I had a decision-making theory, Russ urged me to publish it. In 1984 he requested a simple, illustrated booklet covering a few of the theory's basic points. I disappointed him by producing a short but comprehensive draft, not at all what he had in mind. "Too many new ideas too fast," he said.

Nothing might have come of that draft had not Russ accepted in 1986 the post of editor-in-chief of *Et cetera*, a quarterly journal devoted to the role of symbols in human behavior. As editor, Russ decided that breaking the comprehensive account into pieces might make it digestible. That decision led to the serialized *MacNeal's Master Atlas of Decision Making* reprinted here in book form. I'm also indebted to Russ for granting permission to reprint as commentaries his forewords to the ten *Et cetera* installments.

My most visible debts are to Vince Benedict and Elaine Vogt. Vince served as art director for the ten installments and produced much of the final art. Most of the cartoons, however, were created by Elaine. You can see the great contributions made by these two artists on almost every page.

I thank Susan Milius for gracing this third book of mine (actually the second in order of composition) with her sensitive editorial guidance.

I thank each of the following for commenting on early drafts: Philip R. Bagley, Bernard Baum, Fred Berkobin, Sanford I. Berman, Jay Bernzweig, George Black, Michael J. Brown, H. Boyce Budd, Thomas P. Crolius, Glenda Daker, Dawn Gangwisch, Barbara Graves, Edward A. Handy, Earl Hautala, Caryl Jones, Margot W. Keith, Jeremy Klein, Catherine MacNeal, Priscilla MacNeal, Richard H. MacNeal, Virginia Creed Mattesich, Harry Maynard, Ruth McCubbrey, Emory Menefee, Mary and Lloyd Morain, Melinda S. Peterson, Leonard Ross, Phillip J. Obermiller, Charles Ray Salmon, Madeleine Schroeder, Samuel Shapiro, Thomas Smyth, Richard P. Taylor, Robin Thomas, Joseph W. Wear, Charlotte D. Weiss, and the late William Exton.

I thank Gregory Sawin for his comments on the new pages required for the book version and Paul Johnston for so ably managing the actual book production.

Any errors of style or substance in the final product, of course, remain mine alone.

# Introduction

Only eight years have passed since the final installment in *Et cetera* of this *Atlas*, and yet it already strikes me as the work of a younger man. Had it been reprinted promptly in book form, I might have been tempted to update it a bit. The best course now seems to be to reprint it in as close a form as reasonable to the original, and that's what's been done.

Fortunately, nothing more serious than a continuing flow of implications distances me from the original *Atlas*. Neither its fundamentals—the seven levels, the patterns and linkages within each level—nor its superstructures require revision. So far, they remain just as vital as they were in 1989.

Only decisions deliberately affect events. Understanding decision making, then, would seem a good beginning for most endeavors, including general education. But fifty years of efforts by decision theorists have failed to satisfy the search for a single approach to decision making that could command general assent. Several strong candidates have been championed by various social sciences, business, education, and statistics, but none has been elected as *the* single best approach.

This *Atlas* takes a broader view. It sees each of us as quite properly employing many different decision-making logics. It sees us as the biological inheritors of disparate decision-making logics and of great natural powers to resolve conflicting decisional indicators. Some of these decisional logics, conflicts, and powers were already present in other species. However, human language expanded all three enormously. Language did this, first and oddly enough, by giving the conflicts permanence, and second, by fostering language-based cultures that gave the logics new linkages.

The *Atlas* presents the decision-making logics and linkages in a totally organized manner. It thereby provides a sturdy framework for studying a host of otherwise slippery subjects, such as competence, consciousness, education, error, ethics, humor, linguistic implication, machine translation, power, rationalization, and responsibility, some of which subjects turn up in the later chapters. But, as already noted, it's the relentless flow of these implications that I can't squeeze in here.

None of these further implications need affect your immediate use of the *Atlas*. Its maps are valid, as far as they go, and will help you find your way among deciders and decisions of all kinds. But knowing that the theory has still further and far-reaching implications—that its maps keep inviting new explorations—may add spice to your reading.

**MacNeal's
Master Atlas of
Decision Making**

*Note:*

Read "installment" as "chapter" throughout.

# Commentary one

[EDITOR'S FOREWORD: It is a treat to print herewith by permission the first installment from *MacNeal's Master Atlas of Decision Making*, a book to be published in due course by the International Society for General Semantics. This seminal work extends the basic principles of general semantics farther into so-called value theory than any previous effort.

Sometimes you can't wait, and this is one of those times. We have known for almost three years that Edward MacNeal was preparing a short and illustrated version of his decision-making theories based on general semantics. We were aware that he had tested a token edition in a short course he taught at a school near Philadelphia. We admired his thoroughness. But then we didn't know how much or little time we might have before something forced our hand.

The matter was settled by the unexpected arrival from France of a translation of MacNeal's article "Semantics and Decision Making" (*Et cetera*, Summer 1983), followed shortly by announcements of seminars and a seminar workbook from the same source. (See *Et cetera*, Summer 1987, "Dates and Indexes," for more details.) We had already half-decided to publish *MacNeal's Master Atlas of Decision Making* in serial form, but these new developments clinched the matter. A little competition is a powerful stimulant.

The second paper at the opening plenary session of the 1951 conference on general semantics held at the University of Chicago was MacNeal's "Foundations of a Theory of Decision Making." MacNeal recalls that Charles Morris (who followed him on the program), Irving Lee, and Wendell Johnson all inquired when he intended to publish. Who would have guessed that more than thirty years would pass? This gap between what was already a work several years old in 1951 and general publication in the 1980s accounts for one noticeably odd characteristic of his theory: though it feels new, even strange, yet it is ripe. He, his immediate family, and a few close associates have lived with it for a long time.

Every once in a while a work appears that can change the terms of discussion concurrently in many fields of study and activity. Korzybski's *Science and*

*Sanity* was such a work. It irreversibly altered the discussion of matters relating to language, meaning, and human behavior.

We expect MacNeal's work on semantics and decision making will also change the terms of discussion in many fields, because decision making is so fundamental. Using Korzybskian approaches, MacNeal supplies a rich, coherent, comprehensive, structured, non-elementalistic language for discussing decisions. He identifies levels of decision-making structure that build on each other. He identifies the critical role of recursive (self-reflexive) decisions in world systems. He pinpoints the generic advantages and disadvantages of different decision-making approaches. In short, MacNeal has produced a theory of decision making that consists of successive and exhaustive levels of order, relations and structure that can be tested and that seems to fit our experience.

Korzybski envisioned in 1933 that his analysis would ultimately lead to "a general theory of values" (*Science and Sanity*, 3rd ed. 453). He would probably have expected one of his students to lead the way. MacNeal attended a 1946 seminar. Korzybski would also, we suspect, have been amused that the term "values" itself would have to be dropped as an overworked, multi-ordinal, elementalistic, and hence unsound semantic projection. There's a limit to foresight, Korzybski's or anyone else's.

What seems to have happened since 1933 is that general semantics, as theory, has been regarded and taught mostly as epistemology. As such, it concerns how we know what we know and the limitations of our knowing and communicating. Its students have applied general semantics usefully within and to a great variety of fields. The articles in our journal will bear me out. Clearly, decisions have been and are being affected by general semantics.

However, to the extent that different fields of activity (e.g., law, business, education and politics) employ different decision-making frameworks, we must question whether general semantics hasn't been limited by those frameworks. Doesn't the form of the decision somehow determine the extent to which general semantics can be used?

MacNeal's work escapes such limits by addressing the decision-making frameworks themselves. His *Master Atlas* is not an application of general semantics to decision making in the same sense as past articles have applied general semantics to chemistry or dentistry. It is more like an extension of general semantics. The *Master Atlas* aims to map every variety of decision making within a novel – but semantically rooted and inspired – framework.

This framework appears to provide a better way of describing and classifying decision-making approaches. It appears to offer a new, more encompassing organization that reveals dynamic systems, essential linkages and decision-making patterns in one vast panorama, which lays them more open to semantic analysis.

You may be surprised you didn't discover or develop the organizing principles for this panorama yourself. We have all observed the obviously different decision-making approaches people use – perhaps even in our own delibera-

# Commentary

tions. Yet somehow we usually manage to rationalize and explain these differences away as lapses or as variations that can't be helped or used. This book turns things around. It treats *every* decision-making approach as useful *somewhere* (else why would they all exist?). This book also treats every decision-making approach as potentially dangerous when used incorrectly.

Theories expand in unexpected ways. No one knows quite how one thing will build on another. In tackling these installments, please don't be deterred by a steep step here or there in the climb. The effort is the price of challenging habitual assumptions in unexpected ways. But it is worth it, for the view at the end is big.]

# 1. Groundwork

In a way, Christopher Columbus was dead wrong. His plan called for sailing west 2,400 miles to the Orient. Commissions of experts in 1485 and 1490 had recommended against the voyage, not on any already outmoded flat-earth theory, but on the difficulty of a crossing whose true distance (10,600 miles, Canary Islands to rumored Japan) they had estimated more accurately than he.

Isabella approved the enterprise anyway. She judged the risk ($250,000) as small relative to the potential gains. Besides, what if another sovereign took the gamble and succeeded?*

**Maps and Territories**

When we deliberate about a decision, we deal with maps. Call them "mental maps," or "cognitive maps." They are *our* maps, our *projections* of the decision-action territory.

We can easily forget about the projective character of our maps in a passionate concern for deciding what we are going to do. Yet we can't expect very often to be as fortunate as Columbus, to luck out through ignorance of a map's limitations.

Every map projects a point of view or perspective. Each such projection may serve some uses well even while it introduces other inconveniences or distortions. All maps are selective. That is the nature of maps as representations *different* from what they represent.

---

*Based on Samuel Eliot Morrison's *Admiral of the Ocean Sea*. I have taken the liberty of updating his cost estimate from 1942 (not 1492!) to reflect inflation. [EM]

# Maps and territories

> **MAPS VS. TERRITORIES**
> A map is *not* the territory is represents.
> A map does not represent all of the territory.
> A map may have a structure similar or dissimilar to a structure of the territory.
> An ideal complete map would contain a map of the map, a map of the map of the map, etc., without end.
> (Based on Alfred Korzybski's *Science and Sanity*, 3rd ed., pp. 750-751.)

Take global maps, for example:
1. Mercator's projection permits navigators to set true courses, but falsifies distances and areas. Greenland, in reality smaller than Argentina, looms as large as all of South America.

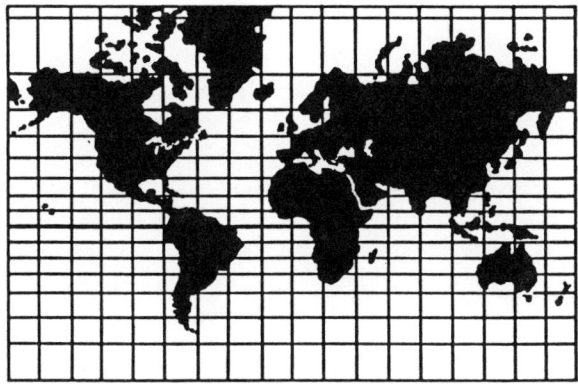

Mercator's projection

2. Mollweide's projection corrects for the areas, but progressively distorts shapes as it recedes from the map's center.

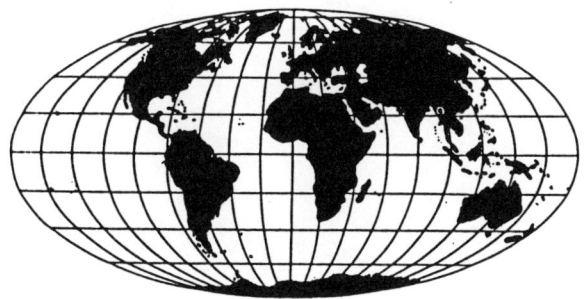

Mollweide's homolographic projection

3. Lambert's equivalent azimuthal projection improves the shapes, but disconnects the hemispheres.

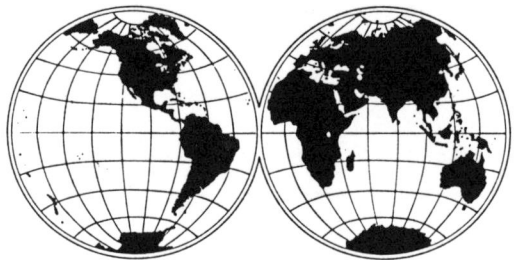

Lambert's equivalent azimuthal projection

4. Goode's interrupted homolosine projection further improves the shapes, but distorts distances by segmenting the world into a flattened orange peel.

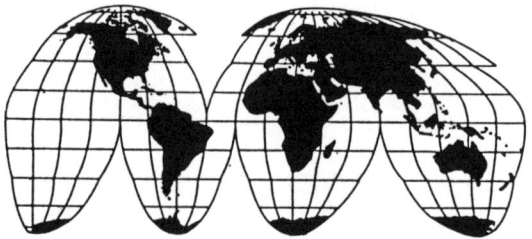

Goode's interrupted homolosine projection

5. A polar equidistant azimuthal projection corrects the distances, but only for one pole, while it deforms the southern continent into a skirt around the entire map.

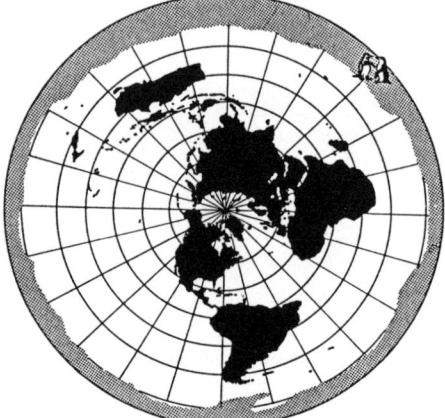

Polar equidistant azimuthal projection

# Decisions and maps

6. A globe reveals "correct" areas, shapes, and distances, but problems of scale, cost, and bulk banish globes from most glove compartments and attaché cases.

## Decisions and Maps

Similarly, we employ many different decision-making map projections.

A decision, for our purposes here, can be defined as "the acceptance or rejection of a course of action."

A decision is the acceptance or rejection
of a course of action

Every decision-making map must allow for representation of the course of action to be accepted or rejected. What else is allowed and how it relates to the course of action in any particular map determines that map's projection. Vice versa, a map's projection determines what kinds of things and relationships can be shown on that map.

We will get into the specifics of decision-making map projections [in the next installment]. All we need do now is establish a general sense of how map projections differ.

Sometimes, like Queen Isabella, we weigh the risks of an action against the potential benefits. Our map must then portray features that can be judged separately from each other, like inputs and outputs, or pros and cons. We employ this projection for many decisions, both in business and in our personal lives.

However, weighing pros and cons is only one of the projections available for decision-making maps.

Weighing the pros and cons

Sometimes, for example, we simply size up a situation and find the action that fits. Then our map need show only the situation and our action in response. For example, the situation we could summarize as "tomorrow is my mother's funeral" has such compelling force that we would not normally weigh pros and cons. We know our proper response is to attend. We also employ this action-to-fit-the-situation perspective in handling many routine business and personal decisions.

Responding with the fitting action

# Decisions and maps 9

In another common decision-making map projection, we see ourselves as working toward a goal. We must then show this goal – perhaps a better grade, higher sales, a better job, or more satisfying personal relationships – on our map. Teams use this projection to promote enthusiasm and cooperative effort toward varied goals – touchdowns, profits, space exploration . . .

Working toward a goal

To take just one more of the many possible examples, we also at times employ the decision-making map projection of previewing alternative futures "non-judgmentally." That is, we reserve judgment while we just try to imagine what each future – perhaps based on a career or a marriage – would be like. Our map in such cases must then show at least two courses of action as the origins of the future worlds we are previewing.

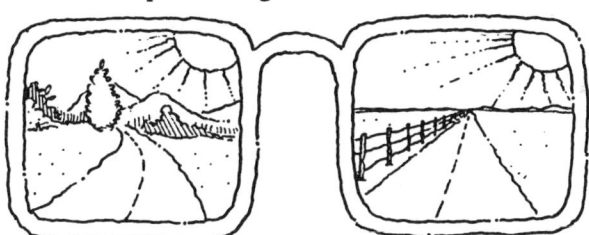

Previewing alternative futures

Thus, like global maps, there is no one perfectly convenient and useful decision-making map projection. No single point of view suits all occasions. Instead, we must use several different perspectives, or projections, in creating our decision-making maps.

> Decision-making map projections affect both conscious and unconscious acceptances (or rejections) of courses of action. This produces a curious no-man's land between deliberate and habitual (or unconscious) choices. Are they all "decisions"? We will return to this question only after exploring all the map projections.

## Three Hazards

We must now face up to three hazards, any one of which could ruin our exploration of decision-making maps.

• Hazard number one is **rationalization.** If Sigmund Freud taught us anything, it was that our ability to disguise our motivations never sleeps. We can all rationalize motivations into forms that suit us better, into our own habitual decision-making map projections. Allowing free rein to such transformations would render our exploration fruitless. We would transform all maps into our favorite one and see nothing to explore.

As you can appreciate, you must, therefore, resist for now the natural urge to reinterpret into your own favorite terms the decisional forms and examples you read here.

This warning applies with special force to older readers, people who have done well in life, and people who for whatever reason feel they "have it made." If your decision-making maps have served you well, you may quite understandably be reluctant to take other perspectives.

Ironically, this hazard holds the greatest danger for social scientists. In addition to the risks already noted regarding natural urges, age, and success, they may also have career investments in particular motivational maps.

I mean no disrespect by suggesting that successful senior social scientists may initially find it difficult to digest what they read here. Their judgments, after all, could ultimately be the most important. I just ask that they resist premature application of their own favorite motivational theories.

We must allow ourselves to acknowledge that we use many decision-making perspectives. Indeed, we have no more reason to insist on consistency in our decision-making maps than in any other tool we use. Nobody in the know expects a geographic atlas to employ only one map projection.* Nor do we expect a carpenter to have only a single, all-purpose tool. Rather, we look for consistency to arise from a reasonably coordinated use of the various drills, saws,

---

*It would be a poor atlas if it did. My old Goode's atlas uses eight projections in addition to the master's own. My National Geographic atlas uses as many as three different projections on the same page and a dozen in all, only two of which appear in Goode's.

# Three hazards    11

and hammers in the chest. And we would look twice at a dedicated driller's criticism of sawyers and hammerers.

• Hazard number two is **clumsy language.** Dictionaries lag far behind our needs. They don't have standard names for decision-making maps. Ordinary terminology, like "decision-making map projections and perspectives," though picturesque, is inexact and cumbersome. For this trip we need a pithy vocabulary.

Let's start right away with the pithy prefix "dema," a contraction of the compound adjective "decision-making." You can pronounce it "DEE-mah" (which I prefer) or "DEM-uh." Either way it just means "decision-making." Use it, however, only as a prefix, as in "demamap" (decision-making map), "demalogic" (decision-making logic), or "demahabits" (decision-making habits). It's a great time and space saver.

decision-making
**de**cision-**ma**king
**de**cision-**ma**king
**de      ma**
**de    ma**
**dema**

Note the term "demalogic." This is the short way to refer to "the particular kind of reasoning that goes with each different kind of decision-making map." Demamaps tend to be static; demalogics are anything but static. A coordinated use of demamaps implies that we know our tools (demalogics) and when to use or not to use each (comparative demalogics). That's where we're headed.

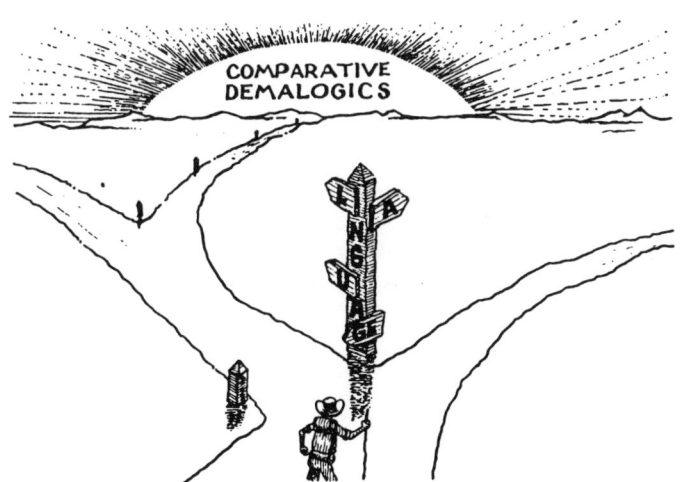

> **HOW DOES COMPARATIVE DEMALOGICS DIFFER FROM OTHER DECISION-MAKING APPROACHES?**
> 1. Comparative demalogics rejects the notion of a universal or "best" demaprocedure.
> 2. Comparative demalogics treats each decision-making approach as a different kind of map useful in some circumstances and not in others.
>
> Many tools help shape our decisions. Why restrict ourselves to one or a few?

> **dema-, demalogic, demalogical, demalogics**
>
> **dema-** \'dē-ma *also* 'dem-ə\ *prefix* [*de*cision-*ma*king]: decision-making
>
> **demalogic** \-'läjik, -jēk\ *n* -s [dema + logic]: any of various modes of reasoning that may be used in making decisions
>
> **demalogical** \-jəkəl, -jēk-\ *adj:* of or relating to demalogic(s)
>
> **demalogics** *n pl but usually sing in constr* [*pl* of *demalogic*] 1: the study of decision-making modes  2: the theory that twenty or so disparate and often unnoticed decision-making modes act as decisional frameworks governing the interpretation and relevance of events, types of error recognized, degree of responsibility, etc., with pervasive effects on human behavior

- Hazard number three is **nearsightedness.** Too often we become preoccupied with our own immediate decisions and mired in our habitual approaches.

Comparative demalogics challenges us to know and select our decision-making tools with care, and to broaden our decision-making skills. We thereby gain more options (both when performing as private individuals and on behalf of organizations), greater understanding of others, and a tool for influencing the decisions others reach.

So let's take a short time-out to see where our decisions fit in the grand scheme of all demalogics. [To be continued. In the next installment: the big, big picture, the most critical decision-making distinctions, and what's so unexpectedly misleading about such words as *action, consequences,* and *values.*]

*Commentary two*

[EDITOR'S FOREWORD: Forty-three years ago, the third issue of the first volume of this journal featured an article by chemist Jerome Alexander titled "Successive Levels of Material Structure" (*Et cetera,* Vol. 1, No. 3, Spring 1944). The present article, were it not the second installment of a larger work, might easily be titled "Successive Levels of Decisional Structure."

Korzybski warned repeatedly that some of our most important terms – like "meaning," "fact" and "truth"– were also among the most complex and troublesome, because they can refer to themselves (e.g., the meaning of meaning) and because they mean different things on successive levels or orders of abstraction. He called these characteristics "self-reflexiveness" and "multiordinality." They give rise to confusion and paradox. (*Science and Sanity,* 3rd Ed. 1, 4, 22, 74, 136, 432, etc.)

In what follows we welcome "decision" into the list of such important and troublesome terms. That we make decisions about decisions cannot be doubted. That an official decision to give up coffee import quotas necessarily involves more complex decisional structures than a personal decision to give up coffee awaits only the recognition of those structures.

General semanticists will accept without question that $decision_1$ is not $decision_2$, but this installment of MacNeal's *Master Atlas* makes a deeper point. Just as Mendeleev and Linnaeus classified elements and life forms into different atomic and biological structural levels, MacNeal here classifies decisions into their different levels of structural complexity. He then names in one table "for those who crave a detailed advance itinerary" the decisional forms he proposes to discuss at each level. I recall no presentation of a multiordinal term as comprehensive and condensed as this table on "decision." Don't expect to grasp its implications all at once.

Korzybski also warned repeatedly of the dangers of elementalism, of splitting verbally what could not actually be split. He cited "space," "time," "matter," "cause," "effect," "body," "mind," "senses," "emotions," "intellect," "fact" and "doctrine," among others, as still creating semantic blockages. (*Science and Sanity*, pp. 30, 87, 93, 106, 243, 380, 545, 719, etc.) He noted that even a term as seemingly harmless as "heat," deemed to be a substance rather than a space-time-matter *event*, had wasted centuries of scientific effort (p. 107).

Our decisional language predates scientific inquiry and our modern abilities to forecast and influence events. This dating helps explain two insidious faults in that language: (1) its lack of succinct terminology distinguishing what we can and what we cannot do anything about and (2) its reliance on terms and predicate structures promoting false-to-fact separations between our actions and their consequences. See "The Flaw," *Et cetera*, Fall 1984.

In spotlighting these faults MacNeal shows again what William Exton extolled as "a penetrating logic for classifying conceptual/evaluative distortions..." (*General Semantics Bulletin* No. 48, review of *The Semantics of Air Passenger Transportation*). To avoid them, the *Atlas* treats space-time-matters as decisional "events," senses-intellect-emotions as "demalogics" (*decision-making* logics), and our action/cause-effects as "alternaquences."

MacNeal tries to make all this seem easy. Maybe he finds it so after nearly 40 years of practice. But you may find – as I did – that ingrained linguistic habit plus intrusive decisional rationalizations (I shall say more about this in the foreword to the next installment) at first get in the way. Don't worry. Keep reading.

For those who missed it, and for those who wish to be refreshed, here is a synopsis of the first installment (*Et cetera*, Summer 1987):

> Our deliberations about decisions involve maps of decision-action territories. Each such map projects a particular point of view. The map is not the decision-making territory, does not represent all the territory, may have a structure similar or dissimilar to the territory, and may contain a map of the map. Different map projections have different uses and dangers. Some quick examples of such projections are weighing the pros and cons, selecting a fitting action, working towards a goal, and previewing alternative futures.
>
> Three hazards immediately threaten to ruin our exploration of decision-making maps: (1) overly-prompt rationalizations, (2) clumsy language, and (3) nearsightedness. Accordingly, (1) readers are cautioned not to convert the discussions and examples into their own favorite decision-making projections. (2) The pithy prefix "dema" (derived from *decision-making* and pronounced either DEEmah or DEM-uh) replaces the compound adjective "decision-making." This permits us to use such terms as "demamap" (decision-making map) and "demalogic" (decision-making logic) in our journey into comparative demalogics. Finally, (3) readers are now asked to look beyond their immediate decisions and habitual approaches, to see where they fit into the grand scheme of all demalogics...]

## 2. More groundwork

**The Big Picture**

The scale of a map determines what relationships it can show. A planetary map can show Earth in relation to Jupiter. A global map can relate Europe to Africa. A city map can relate Central Park to the East River. A suburban property map can show the relation of a main house to its coach house.

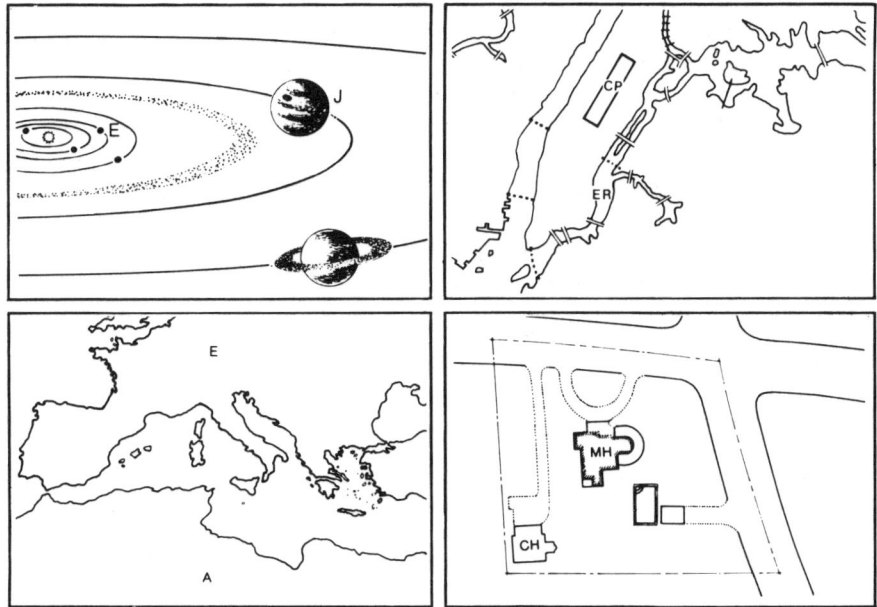

Many fields of study must cover dramatic differences in scale. Physical science addresses structural levels that range from subatomic phenomena to intergalactic collisions. Biological science addresses structural levels that range from intracellular processes to interacting biospheres.

The field of decision making shares this characteristic of physics and biology. Demascience must cover structural levels that range from the mere possibility of consciously scratching an itch to intricately interlaced institutional initiatives in world politics.

Fortunately, several simple distinctions permit us to break this enormous range into convenient structural levels. Level 1, the lowest level, covers *subdecisional events*. Level 2 covers the simplest whole decisions, those whose internal structures reveal only one course of action and no more than one reason. The action and its reason in any such decision always fall into one of five *basic patterns*, from which level 2 takes its name.

Level 3 includes decisions having one action in relation to more than one reason. These fall into various *compound patterns*.

Level 4 covers the *basic linkages* between decisions, those that a single decider could make. Level 5 covers the *interpersonal linkages* between decisions, those that require more than one decider. Level 6 covers self-reinforcing *systems* of interpersonal decisions.

You will find a summary description of each level and one example of its demastructures in the chart at right. Note particularly what each successive step contributes. Level 2 lets in whole decisions. Level 3 adds more reasons. Level 4, more decisions. Level 5, more deciders. Level 6 adds self-reinforcing continuity. And level 7 adds overall review.

Kilroy is there at level 7 to represent comparative demalogics, the taking in of all this. And Kilroy can do it, too, because none of this is difficult, just different from the way Kilroy usually looks at decisions.

Understanding the big picture will help keep each level — and each demalogic within each level — in perspective. If you find at any time that you can't see the demaforest for all the demalogical trees, return to this chapter to reestablish your bearings.

Meanwhile, for those who crave a detailed advance itinerary, here follows a masterchart of all demalogics.

**Table 1    Demalogical masterchart**

| Level | Demalogics |
|---|---|
| Comparative 7 demalogics | comparisons of demalogics at all levels |
| Demasystem 6 | recursive-functionarial-responsive |
| 5 Interpersonal demalinkage | propositional    mutual    reciprocal    organizational enfounding enstaffing functionarial second-order |
| Basic 4 demalinkage | transformative    recursive    quantitative*    allocative |
| Compound 3 demapattern | uniform    multiform    scorecard    sequential |
| Basic 2 demapattern | absolute    responsive    originative action-comparative    goal-directed |
| 1 Subdecisional event | situation    alternaquence course of action consequence |
| *not discussed in this guide. Relax. | |

# The big picture

| | |
|---|---|
| Level 7. Comparative demalogics: comparative study of demalogics at all levels (for example, reading this book) | COMPARATIVE DEMALOGICS **7** |
| Level 6. Systems: self-reinforcing continuities of interpersonal decisions (for example, the socio-economic systems of different nations and now perhaps the efforts of their representatives to reduce conflict) | SYSTEMS **6** — INTERCONNECTED DECISIONS |
| Level 5. Interpersonal linkages: interacting decisions of two or more deciders (for example, one buying and the other selling) | INTERPERSONAL LINKAGES **5** |
| Level 4. Basic linkages: interacting decisions of one decider (for example, how one purchase affects the funds left for other purchases) | BASIC LINKAGES **4** |
| Level 3. Compound patterns: one action in relation to two or more reasons (for example, entering a yard in relation to rain, fierce dog, and package delivery) | **3** COMPOUND PATTERNS — SINGLE DECISIONS |
| Level 2. Basic patterns: one action in relation to one reason (for example, "Put it there; it fits.") | **2** BASIC PATTERNS |
| Level 1. Subdecisional events: events that are not in themselves decisions (for example, rain) | **1** SUBDECISIONAL EVENTS *(To be described in the next chapter)* |

We will start at the bottom, dispose of level 1 in [this installment], and then progress upward. Level 2 will take [one-and-a-half installments]; the basic demapatterns are that important. [Half an installment] will then do for level 3. [Two installments] will be spent on levels 4, 5, and 6, to explore demalinkages [and] demasystems. [The final two installments will present] overviews and angles from the summit of comparative demalogics at level 7.

When Schliemann excavated Troy, he found nine cities piled one atop the other, but only one (on neither level he picked) was the famous Troy of Helen, the wooden horse, and the Trojan war. Our situation is different. All seven of the levels we face are parts of what we know as decision making.

## Level 1: Subdecisional Events — Situations And Alternaquences

Professor Goode called his world map an "interrupted projection." It splits the earth's surface into several orange-peel sections.

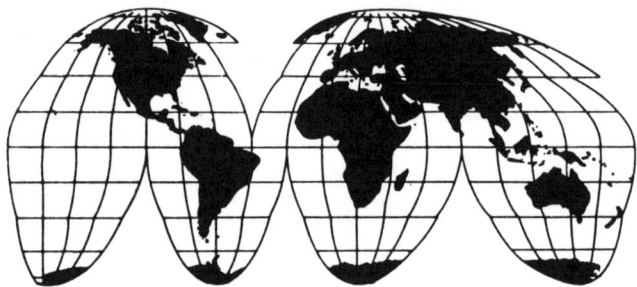

Goode's interrupted homolosine projection

Yet every flat-map world projection is interrupted in one way or another. For example, although the U.S. and the U.S.S.R. face each other across Canada and the Arctic (see the polar projection [in the first installment]), our maps typically place the two superpowers at opposite ends of a "west" to "east" spread. Such maps interrupt the continuity of the earth's surface by splitting it through the polar regions and again in the Pacific Ocean.

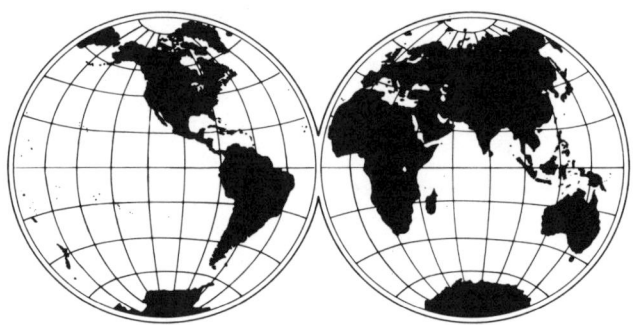

Lambert's equivalent azimuthal projection

# Subdecisional events

When we stop to think about it, we know that the earth's surface is everywhere continuous. Yet we have grown so accustomed to maps with splits and interruptions that they seem perfectly natural.

A similar interruption affects most of our decision-making maps, our demamaps. This interruption yields (as we will see later) both real conveniences and great dangers. I refer to the verbal split between "courses of action" and "consequences." Like the geographic split, this verbal split seems perfectly natural. We effortlessly slice "deeds" or "alternatives" from "outcomes" and "repercussions," because our linguistic maps work that way.

This verbal split permits us to *speak* of "eating" without referring to its health effects, of "buying" without referring to its reducing our monetary resources, and of "rushing a job" without referring to its effects on quality. Wouldn't it be wonderful if the world would follow suit? If we could choose to binge, splurge, and plunge without effect?

When we stop to think about it, we know that actions flow into consequences as automatically as tossed stones make ripples in a pond. Yet no term in common use bridges the verbal split. Indeed, to express the inexorable continuity of action-consequences, we resort to aphorisms. "As you sow, ye are like to reap." "As the twig is bent, the tree's inclined." "They that take the sword shall perish with the sword."

The continued currency of old aphorisms often reflects a terminological shortage. So here's another pithy term for our trip: "alternaquence." One alternaquence, two alternaquences. Just feel how much easier that is on the tongue, once you get used to it, than "course-of-action-together-with-its-consequences-considered-as-an-unsplittable-unit."

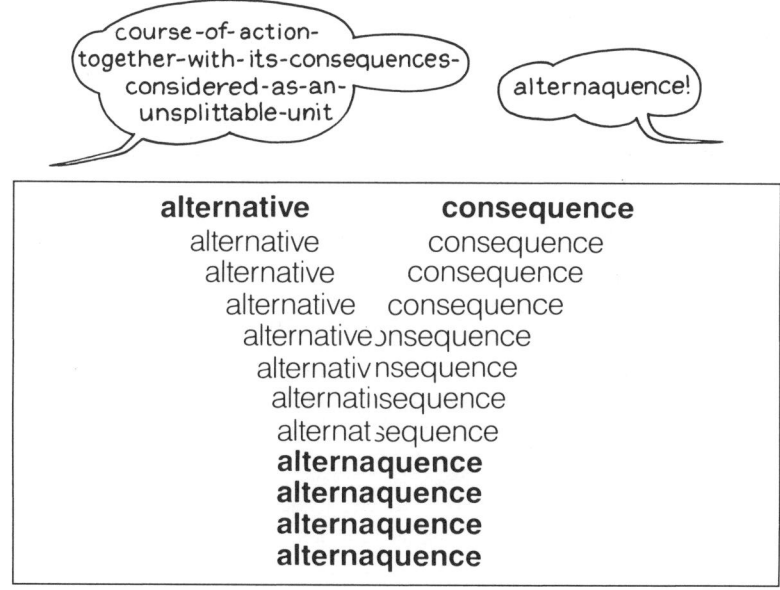

If we cannot in fact take actions without their consequences, what basis might we have for splitting them verbally? Simply that we separate what we are sure we can do from what we are not sure we can do. For example, I can choose to win a race with my three-year-old granddaughter. She, however, can choose only whether to compete. Winning is only a possible consequence for her now, not a surely doable action. In a few years the tables may well reverse.

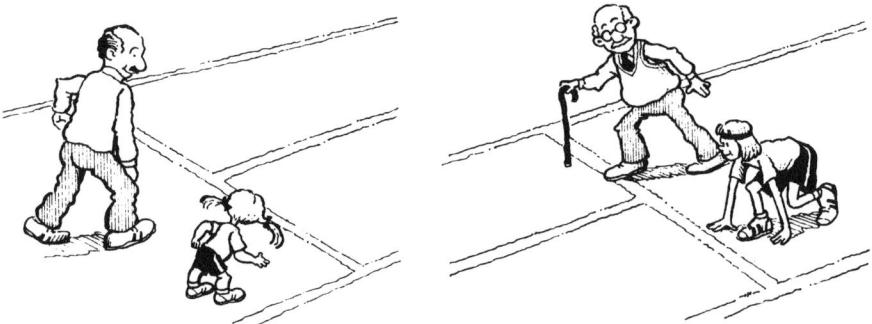

As map symbols for this action-consequence relationship, we will use a triangle pointing to the right for the course of action and a spreading, open-ended, figure with wavy boundaries for the consequences. The dotted line between them represents the artificial verbal split.

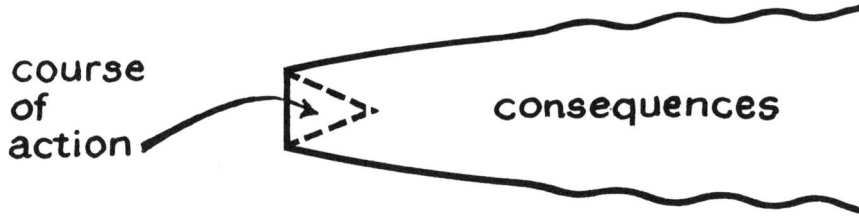

> Alfred Korzybski, the originator of general semantics, attributed many serious misevaluations to the habit of splitting verbally what could not otherwise be split. In his pioneering 1933 work, *Science and Sanity*, he condemned the splits implied by such verbal oppositions as "intellect" to "emotion," and "body" to "mind." In those days people could still be classified as "rational" (presumably a "masculine" trait) or "emotional" ("feminine") without blushing. Diseases were said to be "physical" or "all in one's mind." Korzybski advocated the use of such holistic terms as "semantic reactions" and "psychosomatic" to combat the misleading verbally implied splits.

Another fundamental terminological shortage is revealed by the rapid and enormous popularity of the prayer Dr. Reinhold Niebuhr wrote for a wartime service in the Congregational church of Heath, Massachusetts. Its circulation in its original form runs into the millions.

# Subdecisional events

> ### A DEMAPRAYER
> God, give us grace to accept with serenity the things that cannot be changed, courage to act on the things which can be changed, and the wisdom to distinguish the one from the other.*
>
> *Adapted from Reinhold Niebuhr's *The Serenity Prayer*, 1943. I have changed "change" to "act on" and "should" to "can" to sharpen the underlying demadistinction.

No distinction is more critical for decision making than that between the things we can do or influence and the ones we cannot. Dr. Niebuhr's prayer struck home because he put this distinction so well.

A distinction so welcome and profound surely merits its own pair of names. What, then, shall we call the events that lie on either side of this demaboundary?

We already have the name for the decision-making side. "Alternaquences." The term covers all available actions and their consequences. In short, alternaquences include everything that we could or should change.

The events on the non-decisional side we will call "situations."

Situations include everything we can't change. All things past are situations: yesterday's storm, Marco Polo's China trip, the construction of the pyramids. We can't change those events.

For a reason that will appear in a subsequent chapter, we will diagram a situation as follows:

Events that don't take place may also qualify as situations. It is the situation that the Axis did not win World War II, and that you did not die yesterday.

Tomorrow's sunrise and ocean tides also fall safely on the situational side. We can't change these events either. At least, not yet.

> But once we could begin
> To change this planet's spin,
> Then sunup time and tide
> Would join the demaside.

WHEN WOULD YOU LIKE TO THROW IN YOUR FIRST LINE TOMORROW?

Distinguishing situations from alternaquences has nothing to do with what one likes, wants, or would decide to do. You may decide not to steal, but both stealing and not stealing are alternaquences for you. Anything we *could* do, even if we never do it, and even if we know we never would, lies on the demaside.

Of course, each of us (and each group, and each nation) has a different set of situations and alternaquences. Nobody's choices exactly duplicate anyone else's. And, as already noted, our choices keep changing. What may be unavailable today could well be a choice tomorrow.

To sum up, subdecisional events both in word and in deed split into situations (which lie beyond our deciding) and alternaquences (which we can choose or refuse). Alternaquences, in turn, split verbally, but not otherwise, into actions (which are within our control) and consequences (which are less certainly known but which follow nevertheless).

> Which of the following are alternaquences and which are nondecisional situations for you?
>
> |   | A | S |
> |---|---|---|
> | 1. Burning this book | — | — |
> | 2. Being the author of this book | — | — |
> | 3. Soaking this book in liquid | — | — |
> | 4. Reading #2 again | — | — |
> | 5. Not reading item #5 | — | — |
> | 6. Refusing to classify item #6 | — | — |
> | 7. Being born | — | — |
> | 8. Not reading the whole answer to this question | — | — |
>
> (Answers at end of chapter)

## WHAT ABOUT VALUES?

One need not be opposed to the flag, motherhood, or apple pie to recognize that the term "values" has been overworked. Supermarkets and car dealerships boast of their "values." Morals leaders urge a return to wholesome "values." "Prioritizing one's values" has become a cliché.

The term "values" has come to stand for almost anything of which the speaker approves. Instead of "moral values," "ethical values," "dollar values," "poetic values," and "scientific values," we have just "values," an overstuffed favorable catch-all. This kind of drift is not unusual — look how the neutral term "quality" came to mean "high quality" — but when an implied approval becomes predominant a word's utility for analytical purposes wanes.

We will give "values" a rest.

Instead, we will speak of different kinds of valuing, of different kinds of value judgments, of different ways of relating courses of action to reasons. We will explore the differences between using likes, dislikes, rules, goals, and preferences. In short, we will seek the specifics behind the overworked generality.

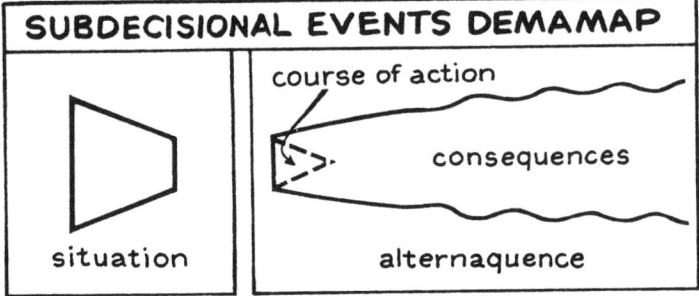

[To be continued. In the next installment: four of the five basic patterns of decision making — the two simplest, the commonest and the most touted.]

### ANSWERS TO THE QUESTIONS ON PAGE 22

1. An alternaquence (unless you find yourself pinned down somewhere without hope of fire).
2. A situation. You are not the author and have no choice in the matter.
3. An alternaquence.
4. An alternaquence (unless you have obliterated it).
5. The situation is that you already have.
6. An alternaquence. It's up to you.
7. A situation. You were born. (Literate robots excepted.)
8. Still an alternaquence to this point, but now a situation.

*Commentary three*

[EDITOR'S FOREWORD: When I first encountered MacNeal's work on decision making I congratulated him for identifying decisional patterns that others ignored. I also wondered how anything so essential to human evaluational practices had escaped my attention. The answer, I now believe, lies in the ease with which we transfer our outlook from one decisional form to another.

Unlike ordinary computers that work only step by step in a single logical chain, our brains use richly interrelated neural nets. Apparently we can process several decisional forms concurrently and not be aware of it. Thus we can shift rapidly from one form to another. For example, we can effortlessly restate a responsive rule ("If the light is red, stop your car") as a goal-directed directive ("To avoid accidents, stop at red lights"). We make this restatement so easily that the difference in the decisional forms ("if x occurs, do y" versus "to get x, do y") usually escapes notice.

MacNeal calls any such shift a transformative linkage. Except for warnings about rationalization, he puts off discussing the linkage until after introducing several decisional forms that could be linked. That sequence makes organizational sense.

I have my own reason for bringing up the transformative linkage this early. As noted in the foreword to the previous installment, linguistic habits and decisional rationalizations initially hindered my grasp of decisional forms. If I had understood at the start how automatic and ordinary those rationalizations were, I might have ignored them better.

It was once thought that imitation fully explained how children acquired language. We now know that our brains are, so to speak, wired for language acquisition. Language comes naturally.

Our brains also appear to be wired for several different decisional forms.

Each form presumably evolved because it confers survival benefits under some but not all circumstances. Having several decisional forms outfits us better for survival. But having more than one decisional form also produces conflicting behavioral indicators. For example, while waiting at an intersection, your responsive network keeps saying, "It's a red light, wait for the green," while your goal-directed network repeatedly urges, "You have to get to the hospital, *go ahead*."

Biologically speaking, the more decisional forms a species has, the more decisional conflicts it will encounter, and the more power of shifting from one decisional form to another it must have developed to resolve the conflicts, or else perish from irresolution. These powers doubtless predate, and are greatly extended by, language. (MacNeal, *Demalogics 2.0*, 1986 token edition, propositions 12.9-12.94.) Such advanced powers make it difficult to hold a focus on one decisional form. And that explains why I failed to notice the forms. I hadn't held still long enough.

MacNeal gives each decisional form a name and specifies its structure in both a formula and a diagram. They can be distinguished operationally and that gets easier with practice. Their divergent behavioral effects can then be appreciated. My advice then? Hold the rationalizations.

For those who missed them, and for those who wish to be refreshed, here is a synopsis of the first two installments (*Et cetera*, Fall and Winter 1987):

> Thinking about decisions involves demamaps, *de*cision-*ma*king *maps*, that project particular points of view. Any such map is not the decision-making territory, does not represent all the territory, and has a working structure (demalogic) determined by the decider's point of view. Some quick examples are weighing the pros and cons, selecting a fitting action, working towards a goal, and previewing alternative futures.
>
> The exploration of decision making requires us to hold our favorite demalogical rationalizations in abeyance while we look at everybody's demalogics from a grander perspective.
>
> We then find seven levels of demalogical structure: (1) subdecisional events, (2) basic demapatterns [in which we relate action to one reason], (3) compound demapatterns [in which we relate action to multiple reasons], (4) basic linkages between decisions [which one decider could make], (5) interpersonal linkages, (6) self-reinforcing systems of interpersonal decisions, and (7) comparative demalogics.
>
> The subdecisional events at level 1 include situations (whatever we can't change) and alternaquences (whatever we can do or influence). Ordinary language splits alternaquences into "actions" and "consequences." This verbal split constitutes a dangerous elementalism. Linguistic presumption aside, we cannot have our actions without their consequences.
>
> We now proceed to level 2, basic demapatterns ...]

# 3. Logics for the single decision

### The Two Simplest Patterns

What is the simplest demamap we could possibly use for a single decision?

As previously defined, a decision is the acceptance or rejection of a course of action. Therefore, at its simplest a demamap must portray at least a course of action. And that is absolutely all it need portray. It needn't include situations, consequences, or other actions. We can accept or reject, like or dislike, a course of action for itself alone. "Coffee?" "No, thank you." (Or "Yes, please.")

We call such decisions — and the pattern into which they fall — "absolute," because they involve acceptance or rejection of a course of action for itself alone. We take or refuse the coffee because, quite simply, we feel or don't feel like having coffee.

Of course, if pressed, we could always *invent* a reason that went beyond our feeling for the action itself. We could say that we accepted the coffee because we were expected to (a situation) or refused it to avoid the jitters (a consequence). But any such invention would instantly invoke a different demalogic and a different demamap. That is why we must for now avoid such rationalizations.

We use the absolute pattern daily in such personal choices as our foods, beverages, bath temperature, and sleeping habits. We find far less use for the absolute pattern in business, because in business — as in sports and school — we typically pursue goals and observe situational rules. How often have you seen "simply doing what you like" as a job description?

Our likes and dislikes can change. Some of the changes reflect our maturing and aging. Do you remember your first taste of unsweetened grapefruit juice? Cheesecake? Beer? Other changes result from random experience. Still other changes result from our conscious efforts to acquire new tastes. We do have a say in whether we will like or dislike grapefruit juice or beer. To some extent we can train ourselves either way.

People often claim they dislike something which they have never tried. How do they know? They just know, right? Wrong. That kind of dislike is something else. It can't be a direct like or dislike for the course of action itself, because it's never been put to the taste test. Their refusal to try involves fear of an unknown result. That's a different demamap; for no consequences appear on an absolute demamap.

The second simplest demamap, the action-comparative, also includes only courses of action, but this time in comparison with each other.

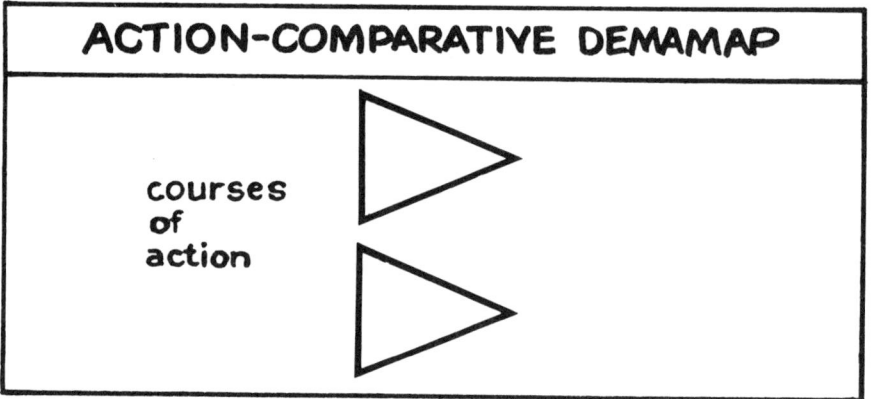

The comparative aspect of action-comparative demamaps makes an interesting difference. It renders likes and dislikes, individually considered, superfluous to the decision at hand. Preference suffices. For example, in choosing between the last two rental cars available, our choice hinges on which we prefer. We may like both cars. We may like neither. Those feelings are superfluous. All we need to know is which car we prefer. Our preference exhausts the choice.

Therefore, deciders in command of both absolute and action-comparative demalogics have an advantage. They need not agonize over those decisions in which every apparent alternative is disliked (or liked). They can put their likes and dislikes aside by shifting their perspective out of the absolute pattern and deciding in the action-comparative pattern, where their preference suffices.

# The commonest pattern

For those who prefer formulas and algorithms to diagrams, the absolute and action-comparative patterns may be summarized as follows.

**Table 2    Two demaformulas**

| Pattern | Formula |
|---|---|
| Absolute | If you like x, do x. |
| Action-comparative | If you prefer x to y, do x. |

Except in directly personal matters, we usually find it difficult to stay within the confines of these two patterns. We introduce other factors and instantly find ourselves in more complex demalogics.

## The Commonest Pattern

The prize for most-widely-used-but-unappreciated demalogic must go to the responsive pattern.

We have defined a basic pattern of decision making as the relationship of one course of action to one reason. In the absolute pattern that one reason is that the decider likes the action for itself; and in the action-comparative pattern, that the decider prefers the action to another action.

The one reason in the responsive pattern is that the action fits the situation. Responsive demalogic reduces the decider's task to identifying the situation and then finding the action that fits.

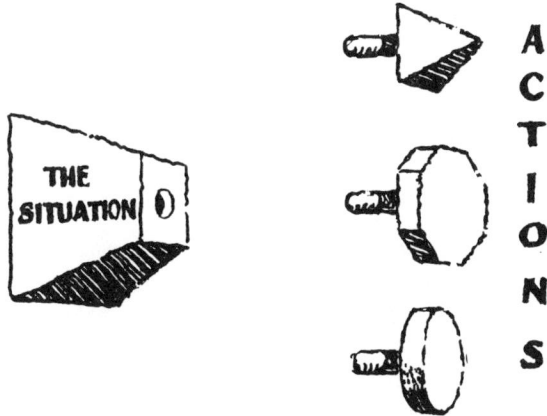

For example, when the alarm goes off (the Situation), we get up (the Action). If it's morning (S), we eat breakfast (A). If it's Monday (S), we head for work (A). If the traffic light turns red (S), we stop (A). Without paying much attention, we respond to situation after situation—stop signs, other cars, other people, elevator doors, and morning "hellos." Some people claim they don't wake up to anything new until they've had their second cup of coffee. Until then, all they need do is recognize the situations and respond fittingly.

Indeed, they might be hard put to define their behavior as decision making. That is one of the benefits—and one of the dangers—of responsive demalogic. We can navigate with responsive demamaps without being aware of them.

A responsive demamap portrays a course of action—as every demamap must—and a situation.

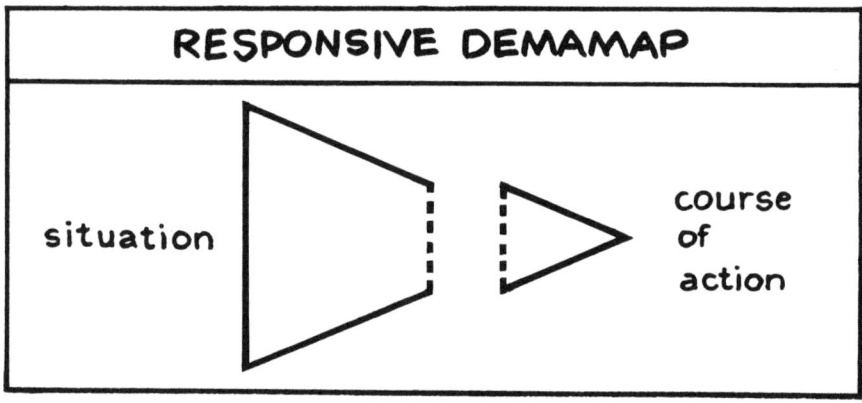

Every culture defines appropriate responses to a great many situations, from what to eat at different times of day and on different days, to how to dress on different occasions, to how to respond to different people, weather conditions, and thousands of other situations. Thus, when these situations arise we share many expectations with other members of our culture, and even more with members of our company, our department, our school, and our family.

These shared expectations of particular responses to specific situations give responsive demalogic a remarkable property. Responsive demalogic permits us to debate actions through true statements that mention neither proposed actions nor consequences. Sounds like an odd debate, doesn't it? Yet we disagree that way repeatedly in responsive demalogic. Here's an example.

### Conversation at a Party

HUSB: It's getting late.
WIFE: This is a great party.
HUSB: We arrived early.
WIFE: No one has left yet.
HUSB: It's been a hard day.
WIFE: I haven't seen Jill in ages.

Each of the six statements describes a situation and each may well be true. True statements can't contradict each other. Yet anyone in our culture would hear in this conversation a disagreement about whether to leave or not. We know without asking that leaving is consistent—for us—with its getting late when we arrived early after a hard day. Just as surely, staying is consistent with its being a great party that no one has left yet, especially when people are there that we haven't seen in ages. If either spouse could win the contest to define the situation, the decision to stay or go would be as good as made. No actions have been mentioned, just implied by responsive demalogic.

Momentous decisions also may rest on how a situation is defined. For example, whether a jury defines the accused's situation as "guilt" or "innocence" is critical to the court's decision and the accused's future.

Responsive demalogic has extremely useful features. A responsive demamap shows no consequences, but enables us to decide by matching actions to situations. This permits us to avoid having to make chancy forecasts. A Federal Aviation Administration inspector, for example, doesn't have to predict the likelihood of a crash, but only to report whether an airline follows the safety regulations. Typists needn't worry about the effects of their assigned letters, but only whether those letters agree with the drafts.

> **RECRUITS' PARODY OF MILITARY TRAINING IN THE RESPONSIVE PATTERN**
>
> 1. If it moves, salute it.
> 2. If it doesn't move, pick it up.
> 3. If you can't pick it up, paint it.

Not having to ponder the effects of our actions saves enormous amounts of time. On job after job, as well as in our private lives, we make decisions faster by following responsive demaformulas.

If we can reduce the definitions of situations and actions to machine language, a computer can make the decisions even faster. Computers run on responsive demalogic.

Table 3     The responsive demaformula

| Pattern | Formula |
| --- | --- |
| Responsive | If x occurs, do y. |

Responsive demalogic also permits consistent human action on a vast scale, coordinations that might never occur if deciders only did what they liked or wanted. For example, all the motorists in a given country drive on the right (or all on the left). Banks accept each other's checks. Different offices of the same company quote the same prices. No large enterprise—be it symphony orchestra, business, or government—could function without responsive demalogic.

Any powerful tool must be used with care. Responsive demalogic—as a tool we use in making decisions—can be dangerous.

The danger of not looking ahead, of not making forecasts, should be obvious. For example, safe driving does not consist merely of following traffic regulations. Sometimes going ahead at a green light is dangerous. Sometimes even stopping at a red light can cause an accident. Safe driving requires a continuing forecast of what pedestrians, other vehicles, your car, and other hazards (animals, rocks, etc.) are likely to do. New configurations and new possibilities keep arising. Reliance on the responsive rules given in traffic regulations works most of the time, but then wham! another unexpected consequence.

### IS THAT REALLY YOU, QUETZALCOATL?

Montezuma, Aztec emperor, believing the Spanish invaders under Cortez to be descendants of the benevolent god Quetzalcoatl, showered them with gifts and received them in November 1519 at his splendid court in Tenochtitlan (later rebuilt as Mexico City). Montezuma was taken hostage by the Spanish and killed within the year. Tenochtitlan and the Aztec empire fell in August 1521.

Some deciders so enjoy the comfort of responsive demalogic that they avoid forecasting as much as possible. Then they go farther and attribute their decision to the situation, as if they had no choice. "He came right out and asked me. I had to tell him." "It was late, I had to leave." To such deciders, their actions are forced by the situation, not really choices at all, and consequences—no matter how unfortunate—were not part of their demamap.

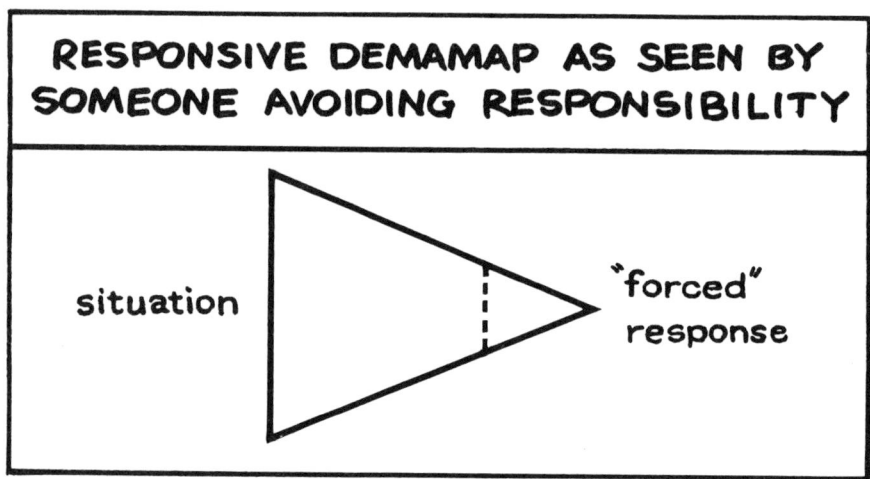

## The Most Touted Pattern

The prize for demalogic-most-often-mistaken-for-the-whole-of-decision-making must go to the goal-directed pattern. Anyone who falls into this trap has plenty of company.

> Every art and every inquiry, and similarly every action and pursuit, is thought to aim at some good; and for this reason the good has rightly been declared to be that at which all things aim.
> Aristotle, *Nichomachean Ethics*, c.330 B.C.
>
> Many different approaches to the decision problem converge on one particular model.... The decision-maker wants to achieve something — call it his goal, purpose, objective, or any other synonymous word.
> Miller and Starr, *The Structure of Human Decisions*, 1967.

However, to see decision making plainly, we must avoid rationalizing all behavior into the goal-directed pattern. We must avoid inventing hidden purposes for every act. The city clerk who refused to help us may only have been following responsive rules. The friends who left us to go swimming may only have been doing what they liked.

Once we stop trying to make goal-directed demalogic account for everything, we can see it better as just one of several basic patterns; important, but limited.

Like all basic patterns, the goal-directed involves a single reason for the acceptance or rejection of one course of action. The reason in the goal-directed pattern is that the action leads (or does not lead, in the case of rejection) toward a particular desired consequence, the goal.

A goal-directed demamap, therefore, shows both a course of action and a particular desired consequence.

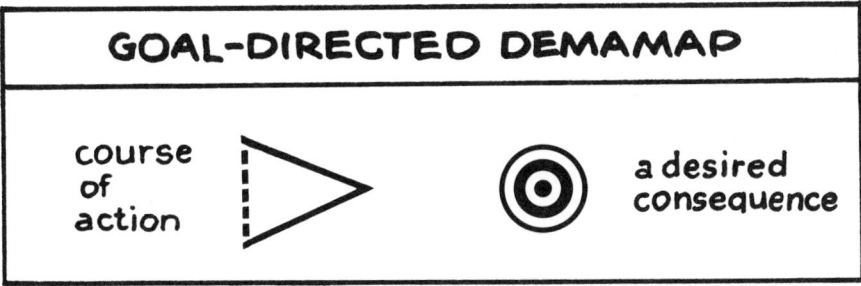

Goals are desired consequences. Like all consequences, the actual achievement of a goal suffers from at least some uncertainty. (Otherwise, remember, we would have a sure thing, a choosable course of action.) Great goals — like peace, or the eradication of disease — may carry great uncertainty.

Our task as goal-directed decision makers is to reduce the uncertainty by finding actions that lead to, or at least closer to, the goals. Perhaps when we find actions that we can depend on, we will transform them into responsive rules. Until then, however, we—like Columbus—must venture beyond certainty's edge.

The goal-directed demalogic helps marvelously by focusing our energy and attention. We wake up with new ideas and determination. We find new sources of strength and endurance.

Goal-directed demalogic permits enthusiastic cooperation by vast groups. Thousands can work together building highways or strengthening levees. Millions can join together to defend themselves against disease or tyranny.

All this power stems from a remarkably simple demalogic, a formula that focuses energy and imagination like no other.

**Table 4     The goal-directed demaformula**

| Pattern | Formula |
|---|---|
| Goal-directed | To get x, do y. |

Every demalogic, however, has it dangers and limitations. The goal-directed pattern is no exception.

One danger of the goal-directed pattern arises from the ease with which it leads to extremes. Goals not only focus attention, they hypnotize. In the words attributed to Vince Lombardi, then coach of the Green Bay Packers, "Winning isn't everything, it's the only thing." Or, more tragically, in the words attributed to an American officer firing on Ben Tre, Vietnam, "It became necessary to destroy the town in order to save it." This danger was described about 1,600 years ago by St. Jerome as that "of justifying the means by the end."

Another danger known to all who use the goal-directed pattern is failure. As goals are consequences, their achievement must by definition admit of some uncertainty, some chance of failure. The true devotees of the goal-directed pattern welcome the risk. In Gilbert's line, which some do in; "Nothing ventured, nothing win." Others, however, shrink back out of fear of failure.

The major limitation of the goal-directed pattern arises from its chief virtue, its ability to concentrate attention and energy on a desired consequence. By spotlighting one particular consequence, goal-directed demalogic consigns all other consequences to the shadows.

From the shadows emerge surprises. From insulating with asbestos to REDUCE FIRES, lung cancer. From taking thalidomide to REDUCE TENSION, deformed offspring. From dumping wastes to IMPROVE INDUSTRIAL EFFICIENCY, a polluted environment. From the cost of emission controls to CLEAN UP THE ENVIRONMENT, unemployment.

Some effects that emerge from the shadows—like those of the pesticides that threatened to create a "silent spring"—ultimately overshadow the original goal. But to gain that primacy, these effects must first endure a second-class status,

# The most touted pattern

that of *side effects*. Since effect is an effect is an effect, the demeaning status of "side" effect merely reflects our preoccupation with goals. The preoccupation acts as a kind of prejudice that confers esteem on our goals and neglect on the other consequences of our acts.

One can even imagine a world peopled with sincere goal-directed deciders, each of whom nevertheless must struggle with the side effects of the others' decisions. Think, for example, of encountering a parade while crossing Manhattan by taxi during truck delivery hours on the fifth day of a summertime garbage collectors' strike.

We slip into goal-directed demalogic more easily than we expect. All it takes is a word, any of a great many words. For example, take the word "problem." The moment we utter or think it we deliver ourselves directly into the goal-directed pattern. A problem begs a solution, and "solution" is another name for goal.

> [W]hat is the relation of decision processes to problem solving? We see these two as much the same, and use the concepts interchangeably...
> [T]he actual satisfying...object or event...we call the goal or the end...
> Brim *et al., Personality and Decision Processes,* 1962.

Equating decision making with problem-solving, then, provides another way to mistake the goal-directed pattern for the whole field.

**Table 5    A sampling of goal-directed words**

| Subject | Words |
|---|---|
| Desired consequence | aim, goal, target |
| What's lacking | deficiency, need, requirement |
| Desire | ambition, longing, purpose |
| Laying out action | design, plan, scheme |
| Overall plan | campaign, crusade, strategy |
| Person used | accomplice, agent, helper |
| Thing used | means, resource, tool |
| Going into action | perform, strive, try |
| Difficulty | hurdle, obstacle, problem |
| Quality of effort | aimless, purposeful, tenacious |
| Ineffective effort | defeat, fiasco, loss |
| Effective effort | achievement, triumph, win |
| Calculated effect | expected, foreseen, intended |
| Unplanned effect | accident, side effect, surprise |

[To be continued. In the next installment: the final two decision-making patterns in the *Atlas,* the *sleeper* and the *scorecard,* the one the most holistic and the other the most deliberately fragmented of all demapatterns.]

## Commentary four

[EDITOR'S FOREWORD: One potential disagreement I have with MacNeal lies in his choice of examples.

As editor of a journal, I would like him to use more exciting and topical examples. Articles on religious wars, messes in Washington and sexually transmitted diseases attract readers. Even a journal going strong in its forty-fifth year likes to attract readers.

As a decision theorist, MacNeal sticks mostly to simple examples that make clean distinctions. Traffic lights, mothers' birthdays, unsweetened grapefruit juice, when to leave a party, crossing Manhattan by taxi during rush hour, that sort of thing. He tells me that issue-ridden examples polarize readers and make decisional logics harder to grasp. He cites the hazards numbered one and three (rationalization and nearsightedness) from our first installment (*Et cetera*, Fall 1987). He even threatens to delay an installment of the *Master Atlas* while he pens an article to be titled "The Issue Issue," if I champion juicier examples.

Okay. Peace. Others of us will have to show later how relevant the *Master Atlas's* decisional approaches are to current debates.

Meanwhile, the present installment poses a neat "issue" of its own. Two decisional patterns are presented: the originative and the scorecard. The originative is our most holistic pattern ("non-elementalistic" in Korzybskian terms). The scorecard is our most fragmented ("elementalistic") pattern. Even so, MacNeal insists that each pattern has its own uses and dangers, so that the issue reduces to when to use each. He offers neither pattern as "the approach" to all decisions. He has admitted elsewhere, however, that he prefers the originative approach for tough decisions (see "When Does Consciousness of Abstracting Matter the Most," *Et cetera*, Spring 1986). So a non-elementalistic decisional approach does have some particularly important uses. Should a general semanticist settle for any less?

Once again, here is a synopsis, this time of the first three installments (*Et cetera*, Fall 1987 through Spring 1988):

> In making decisions, we use various demamaps (*de*cision-*ma*king *maps*) that are not the decision-making territory, do not represent all the territory, and have working structures (demalogics) determined by each decider's point of view. Some examples are weighing the pros and cons, selecting fitting actions, working toward goals, and previewing alternative futures.
>
> To explore decision making, we need to put our favorite demalogical rationalizations aside while we look at demalogics from a grander perspective.
>
> We then find seven levels of demalogical structure: level (1) subdecisional events, (2) basic demapatterns [one action for one reason], (3) compound demapatterns [one action for multiple reasons], (4) basic linkages between decisions [which one decider could make], (5) interpersonal linkages, (6) self-reinforcing systems of interpersonal decisions, and (7) comparative demalogics.
>
> The subdecisional events at level 1 include situations (whatever we can't change) and alternaquences (whatever we can do or influence; from *alter*native and conse*qences*). The verbal split between "actions" and "consequences" constitutes a dangerous elementalism, because the linguistic presumption fails; we cannot have our actions without their consequences.
>
> Four of the five basic demapatterns at level 2 incorporate this dangerous elementalism.
>
> | Demapattern | Formula |
> | --- | --- |
> | absolute | If you like action x, do x. |
> | action-comparative | If you prefer action x to action y, do x. |
> | responsive | If situation x occurs, do action y. |
> | goal-directed | To get goal x, do action y. |
>
> We ordinarily use the first two patterns only for simpler personal matters and we generally fail to notice that we use responsive demalogic the most. Therefore, we sometimes talk as if goal-directed demalogic was all we had.
>
> Each of these four elementalistic demalogics mixes great utility with great danger by permitting all or most consequences to be ignored. Thus our personal bodily tastes, our rules for proper behavior, and our blindered strivings can both serve us well and lead us astray.
>
> We come now to the fifth, and as it happens, our only non-elementalistic demapattern . . .]

# 4. More logics for the single decision

**The Sleeper**

If awards were given for such things, the one for *least* recognized demalogic would go to the originative pattern.

The originative pattern is simplicity itself, but not automatically easy, because its form is not built into the language the way responsive and goal-directed patterns are. Let's define it in two easy stages, starting with the action-comparative pattern.

We all use action-comparative demalogic, decision by direct comparison. "I prefer chocolate to vanilla." "I'd rather sit here than go for a walk." No goals, no fitting to situations, not even likes and dislikes for individual actions. (Indeed, we might dislike both chocolate and vanilla.) Just a direct comparison of actions and a decision for the one we'd rather experience.

Now, extend that direct comparison to alternaquences. "All in all, I'd rather move to Indiana with the company than quit and stay here. After thinking through how each way might go and sleeping on it, it's clear to me which I prefer." No goals, no fitting to situations, no likes or dislikes for individual actions or consequences. Just a direct preference for living through one alternaquence rather than another.

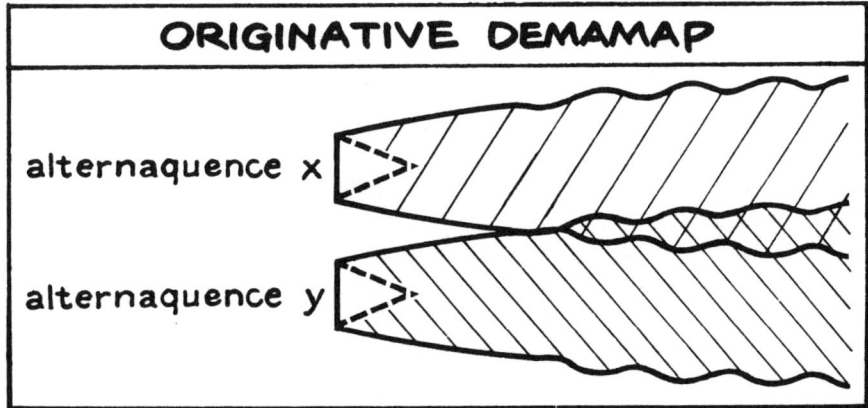

Of course, nothing forces us to omit goals, situations, likes and dislikes from our demamap. But to argue that we *could* include them — or even that we usually do — misses the point that we needn't include them, and in originative demamaps, we don't.

| Table 6 | The originative demaformula |
|---|---|
| Pattern | Formula |
| Originative | If you prefer alternaquence x to alternaquence y, do x. |

If the originative pattern is unrecognized and unsung, much of the oversight flows from our lack of terminology. Unlike the goal-directed pattern, which we can summon with a single word ("purpose," "problem," "need," and many more), we have few words that invoke the originative pattern. "Options," "prefer," "I'd rather," and "all in all" almost exhaust the ordinary list, and the first three must be shared with the action-comparative pattern. Even the unit of choice in an originative decision, the alternaquence, falls outside most vocabularies.

At a deeper level, the very structure of our English verbs, with their three separate time realms—past, present, and future—tends to undermine the originative approach. Speakers of English and most European tongues live with constant linguistic pressure to split alternaquences into a present action and future consequences.

To exploit alternaquences we need another time sense, a sense of continuous flow, a sense that tomorrow is not so much *another* day as a *later* time. There is nothing mysterious about this sense. As the insurance-executive-turned-American-Indian-linguist Benjamin Lee Whorf pointed out, "Languages by the score get along well with [just] two tenselike forms answering to this paramount relation of 'later' to 'earlier.'" But only a few readers of this Atlas will know a language (Hopi, for example) that automatically requires them to take into account that 'later' always retains the accumulated effect of actions taken 'earlier.'*

---

**GLOBES AND ORIGINATIVE DEMAMAPS**

An originative demamap shows alternaquences the way a globe shows the earth's surface—as *continuous.*

An originative demamap shows rival alternaquences the way a globe shows continents—in proper relation to each other.

Like any map, of course, an originative demamap
— is not the action-territory it represents
— does not represent all the territory
— is inconvenient for many uses

---

To think originatively, we must ward off the demalogics attending so many innocent-sounding words. Such common terms as "father," "boss," "duty,"

---

*"To the Hopi . . . time is not a motion but a 'getting later' of everything that has ever been done, [even] unvarying repetition is not wasted, but accumulated." Whorf, Benjamin Lee, "The Relation of Habitual Thought and Behavior to Language." *Et cetera,* Summer 1944.

# The sleeper

"beautiful," "disgusting," "problem," "goal," "purpose," "wasteful," "efficient," and at least a thousand more, presume their own non-originative demamaps. To the uninitiated, such words function almost magically—if unintentionally—as incantations casting out the originative approach.

Yet originative demalogic offers an unusual advantage for certain critical decisions. We need not judge whether we find any action or consequence in itself good or bad in any sense, but only which of the unsplittable alternaquences we find preferable. We thus avoid bedeviling ourselves with the contradictions inherent in looking first at a rule, then at a goal, then at a like or dislike, etc. Yet we can still take into account our best preview of what life would be like following various courses of action.

Take, for example, a situation ordinarily loaded with goals and responsive rules, say, when you are first questioned about something only you know you broke. Tension could set in between your goal of staying out of trouble and the rule that one must in any situation tell the truth. As an originative decider, however, you would focus on alternaquences. You could start by noting that the truth might bring the matter to a head and confirm your honesty, while a lie might reduce your credibility indefinitely.

Whatever an originative decider chooses to do, there is no way from that act alone for an outside observer to tell that it resulted from looking at alternaquences. Honesty could still look like adherence to a rule about truth. A lie could still look like fear of a rebuke.

Originative demalogic permits us to transcend rules, goals, and tastes in the face of circumstances. We can reach a decision even when *every* choice—looked at in other demapatterns—appears wrong or dangerous. We must first, however, get past a reluctance to think in terms of alternaquences.

## TURNING POINTS*

### I. Words

Oh may we not, sir, please dispense
With, ugh, the term "alternaquence"?

---

*Reprinted from "Semantics and Decision Making," *Et cetera*, Summer 1983, with first-line typo corrected.

For in the present I would live
And stick to plain "alternative."

That deeds have outcomes, yes, I've heard,
And know it well without that word.
Make up a term to please the ear
That's short, or sweet, or needed here.

You'll find me then among the first
To take it up. But your's the worst.
I pray you, sir, avoid offense.
Abandon now "alternaquence."

II. Decisions

Nothing brings me to my senses
Like previewed alternaquences.
Knothole gapes reveal profusions,
Rules, my tastes, my goals, confusions.

Wire-walking on high fences
Barbed with acts and consequences,
Dare I style so goal-directed
Sequelae flow side-effected?

Shall I social signals stack, so
All presume I just react? Oh,
Off, pretenses! Out, defenses!
Come, my live alternaquences.

Poems aside, however, to suit today's conventions originative deciders usually stay in the closet.

The danger—both real and imagined—of originative demalogic lies in abandoning rules, goals, tastes, and other specialized demamaps needed for fast action and social coordination. We might agree that a brilliant originative group could be highly useful in brainstorming actions for a truly unprecedented development—say an ice age coming in five years or the receipt of an ultimatum from the bees on behalf of all pollinating insects. Yet even originative deciders, if their own houses were on fire, would presumably send for the regular goal-directed, responsively drilled, team of fire fighters.

**The Scorecard Pattern**

What happens when we use more than one reason to select a single course of action? Plenty.

First of all, we move away from the simplicity and clarity that go with each basic demapattern taken one at a time.

# The scorecard pattern

**Table 7**      **The basic demapatterns**

| Pattern | Formula |
|---|---|
| Absolute | If you like x, do x. |
| Action-comparative | If you prefer x to y, do x. |
| Responsive | If x occurs, do y. |
| Goal-directed | To get x, do y. |
| Originative | If you prefer alternaquence x, to alternaquence y, do x. |

Once we employ two or more reasons in a single decision we enter structural level 3, the level of compound patterns. (See [the second installment] for the big picture.) If our compound pattern incorporates opposing reasons – the usual case – then we have a decision in the scorecard pattern.*

A scorecard decision takes the reasons that would have ended deliberation in a basic pattern and reduces them to points pro and con to be weighed. Our likes, dislikes, preferences, rules, and goals become just so many items to be weighed in the balance.

**Table 8**      **Two scorecard demaformulas**

| Pattern | Formula |
|---|---|
| Scorecard 1 | If x's good points outweigh it's bad points, do x. |
| Scorecard 2 | If x's net score beats y's net score, do x. |

The simplest kind of scorecard map, demalogically speaking, occurs when the points pro and con can all be transformed into values on the same numerical scale. An example would be a business decision on whether to buy or lease a machine. The calculations may get complicated, but initial cash outlay, depreciation, tax effect, maintenance responsibility, residual value, etc., can each be translated into dollars and then combined into a bottom-line figure. Many business decisions fit this model.

---

*Other compound patterns: the uniform has concurring reasons in the same pattern; the multiform has concurring reasons in different patterns; the sequential breaks decisions into steps allowing different patterns in turn.

Scorecard maps become demalogically complex when the reasons to be combined derive from different demapatterns. For example, in choosing a college, we may feel a responsive attachment to a parent's alma mater, a goal-directed desire to start our career in the best school for our field, an absolute liking for the life style of still another college, and a simple preference for not going too far from home.

Our demamap starts to show many situations ("Our family has always gone to Yale;" "Cal Tech has the best department;" "Penn is so convenient;") and many consequences. Some of the consequences (like career prospects) may relate to goals; others (like the loosening of hometown ties, meeting new people, and developing new tastes) may not.

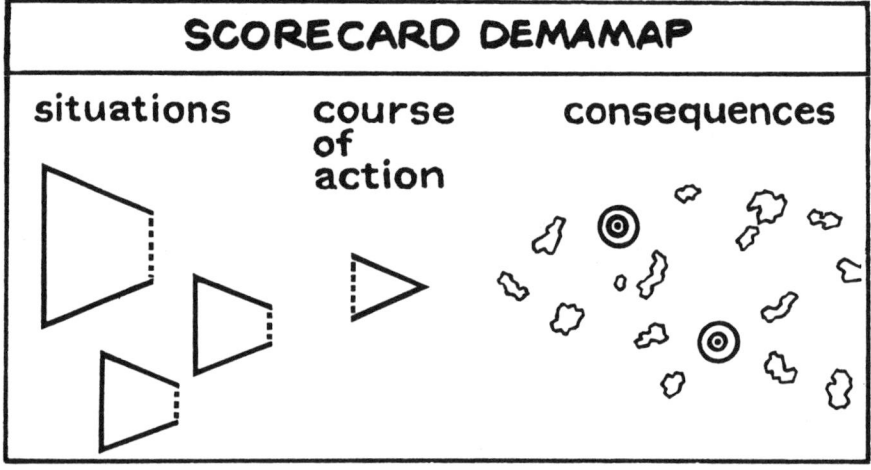

Our scorecard demamap, in effect, contains many different map projections. They tend to slip and slide past each other. Have you ever been frazzled when trying to find the right road map while lost and driving alone in heavy traffic? And how about when the road maps don't agree with each other?

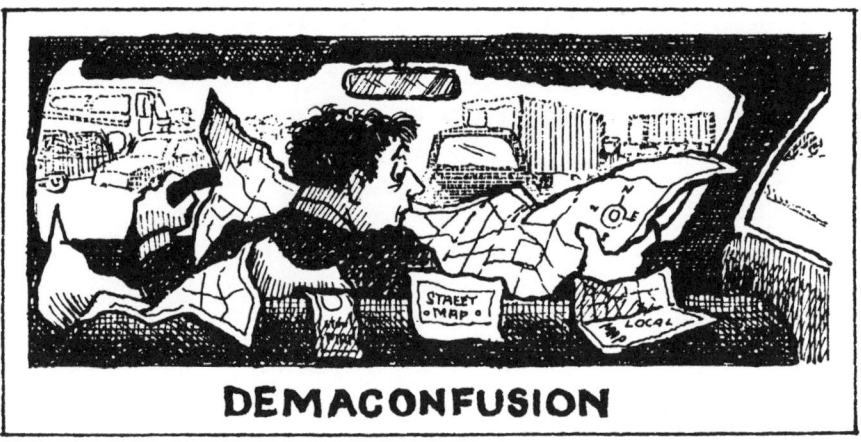

# The scorecard pattern

At that point we need to realize that all contradictions arise from mapping, from our symbolizing the territory. The territory alone, no matter how painful or confusing to our senses, contains no contradictions.

For example, a bull alligator occasionally devours his own offspring. Such unfinicky eating runs counter to our responsive map of how fathers should treat their children and our goal-directed map of procreation for the purpose of perpetuating one's line.

To say that the alligator's behavior is contradictory, then, means that his behavior offends our maps, not that the alligator's behavior contradicts itself. Take away the maps, and the alligator's behavior is just what he does, neither consistent nor contradictory.

Our action maps frequently contradict each other. ("An eye for an eye." "Turn the other cheek." "I want to buy a car, but the money was saved for my education.") The more maps, the greater the chance for contradiction.

Scorecard deciders stride right into this potential confusion. They treat each map as having partial validity, assign it a weight, and move to the next map. Their final decision will depend on the collected weights of all the reasons considered.

Scorecard maps play a large role in business decisions and wherever a multitude of individually inconclusive factors can be summarized on a single scale. Scorecards work especially well where the scale represents a standard quantifiable criterion (such as profitability in a business or lives saved by medical procedures).

Scorecard maps often work reasonably well even when the individually inconclusive factors don't convert easily into values on a single scale. Picking a college, an apartment, a job, or a vacation spot may be examples, provided the decider has no overriding interest in each case.

The main challenge of scorecard decisions lies in converting likes, dislikes, preferences, rules, and goals into units that can be added and subtracted. Both detachment and comfort in relying on calculations will help meet the challenge.

One danger of scorecard demalogic lies in losing the benefits of other demalogics. Reducing "Thou shalt not kill" to an "8" or "9" on a scale from

1 to 10 loses something. To say that "everything is relative" has a nicely old-fashioned Einsteinian ring to it, but too glibly dismisses other approaches.

The interrupted character of the scorecard demamap poses another danger. We may score bits and pieces, and overlook the synergy of the whole. Thus, because we have separate aversions to old milk, milk that has separated, and infestations by bacteria or mold, we could fail to appreciate their combination. Cheese, anyone?

---

**WHICH DEMAPATTERN WOULD YOU USE?**

If you could use the six demapatterns we have now described (absolute, action-comparative, responsive, goal-directed, originative, and scorecard) just once each, which would you use for these six circumstances?
1. Your telephone is ringing................... _____
2. An airline reservations clerk asks whether you prefer a window or aisle seat ....................... _____
3. Your two-year-old child has just fallen in the lake. _____
4. You are sixty and have just received a reasonable offer to buy your company ....................... _____
5. You are offered a second helping of creamed spinach _____
6. You have located a new home that might suit you.. _____

(Answers at top of page 60)

---

This ends the exposition of how people relate an action to reasons within one decision. In the next chapter we move to a new level of decisional structure. [To be continued. In the next installment: three decisional linkages for the lone decider—the slipperiest, the most vital, and the least avoidable.]

## Commentary five

[EDITOR'S FOREWORD: My first excursion into MacNeal's decision theory was through a still unpublished manuscript that dealt primarily with the action-reason patterns within decisions and only secondarily with other matters. I confess that I found the patterns more personal and fascinating than the rest. I attempted to persuade MacNeal to concentrate on the patterns.

MacNeal, however, was inclined otherwise. The patterns were old stuff to him. He was fascinated by how they formed a foundation for other things. Gradually these other things took shape, becoming decisional linkages and dividing into four structural levels. They completed the seven levels of decisional structures covered in the *Master Atlas*. See table 1 in the second installment, *Et cetera*, Winter 1987.

I still find the patterns more personal. I am glad that the latter part of the present installment consists of an extended example of four patterns in confrontation in a factory conference room. Yet I now realize that my understanding of such an example depends on my knowledge of and experience with the decisional linkages involved. No decision exists in isolation. Each relates to others through one or more of several types of linkage.

Some patterns and linkages reinforce each other more than others. Bureaucracies breed institutionalized responsive patterns. Efficiency depends usually on how one goal-directed decision affects another. Organizational linkages tend to discourage originative (holistic) decisions. It follows that patterns and linkages must be studied together for most purposes. Most improvements in decisional skills at the pattern level, for example, must overcome in one way or another the effects of the surrounding decisional linkages. We cannot change the world just by changing how each of us uses the patterns in our own decisions. We also need to forge new linkages.

Once again, here is a synopsis, this time of the first four installments (*Et cetera*, Fall 1987 through Summer 1988):

In making decisions, we use various demamaps (*de*cision-*ma*king *maps*) that are not the decision-making territory, do not represent all the territory, and have working structures (demalogics) determined by each decider's point of view. Some examples are weighing the pros and cons, selecting fitting actions, working toward goals, and previewing alternative futures.

When we get past our favorite demalogical rationalizations we find seven levels of demalogical structure: level (1) *subdecisional events*, (2) *basic demapatterns* [one action for one reason], (3) *compound demapatterns* [one action for multiple reasons], (4) *basic linkages* between decisions [which one decider can make], (5) *interpersonal linkages*, (6) self-reinforcing *systems* of interpersonal decisions, and (7) *comparative demalogics*.

Subdecisional events (level 1) include *situations* (what we can't change) and *alternaquences* (what we can do or influence, from *altern*ative and con*sequences*). Verbally splitting "actions" from "consequences" produces a dangerous elementalism. The linguistic presumption fails; we cannot have our actions without their consequences.

Four of the five basic demapatterns (level 2) and both versions of the major compound demapattern (level 3) exhibit this dangerous elementalism. Only the originative pattern avoids it.

| Demapattern | Formula |
| --- | --- |
| absolute | If you like action x, do x. |
| action-comparative | If you prefer action x to action y, do x. |
| responsive | If situation x occurs, do action y. |
| goal-directed | To get goal x, do action y. |
| originative | If you prefer alternaquence x to alternaquence y, do x. |
| scorecard 1 | If x's good points outweigh its bad points, do x. |
| scorecard 2 | If x's net score beats y's net score, do x. |

We ordinarily use the first two patterns for simpler personal matters, fail to notice that we use responsive demalogic the most, and tend to talk as if goal-directed demalogic was all we had. Our normal, linguistically encouraged, adherence to elementalistic "values" bars usage of the originative pattern and promotes the scorecard.

Each pattern has its own uses and dangers. Some patterns allow most or all consequences to be ignored. Some hamper prompt conventional response and coordination. Each offers only a specialized way of relating actions to reasons.

The *Master Atlas* will explore demapattern uses and dangers further in later installments. First, however, we need to explore additional levels of demalogical structure. . .]

# 5. Logics for interconnected decisions

At this point we leave our consideration of single decisions and move on to interconnected decisions. (A glance back at table 1 [in the second installment] would be in order.) We begin with level 4, where we start connecting decisions (or demapatterns) to each other.

**The Slippery Link**
We can link decisions or demapatterns to each other in many ways. The slipperiest is the reformulation of decisions in a different demalogic, the exchange of one demamap for another. These linkages identify transformative demalogic at work.

**Table 9**   **The transformative demalinkage**

| Demalogic | Identifying Linkage |
|---|---|
| Transformative | conversion of a decision from one to another demapattern |

The cardinal principles of transformative demalogic are:
1. Any action that could be chosen in any demapattern could also be chosen in any of the others.
2. No observer can know for certain what demapattern anyone else has used.

For example, you might decide to beg off a trip you had half agreed to take with a friend. You could then present your decision to your friend in any demapattern.

absolute – "I really don't feel like going. I just wouldn't enjoy it."
action-comparative – "I would rather make it another time."
responsive – "My uncle is visiting us, so I have to stay around."
goal-directed – "I must study so that I can get a good grade."
originative – "Things will probably turn out more to my liking if I practice than if I go off this weekend."
scorecard – "I'd still like to go, but there are just too many reasons not to."

Each demapattern casts your decision in a different light. Which you choose to express probably depends on more than just how you reached your decision. You might consider how your friend will react and what your choice will reveal about your decision-making habits.

Note that each of these demapatterns provides a plausible explanation of your decision. Your friend cannot safely label any of them as "made up." This makes any theory about behavior a very tricky business. Perhaps the surest fact is that a lot of us are good rationalizers. That is, on the personal level at least, we know a lot about how to use transformative demalogic.

We can also use transformations more openly to get the advantages of a different demapattern. For example, as a consultant I often find that clients have reasonable goals but need to translate them into responsive rules that everyone can follow. At other times I find managers who make individually good decisions (in the responsive, originative, or scorecard patterns) but who need to identify the goals those decisions serve in order to bring more resources to bear. I have also found managers so hypnotized by their goals that they need a fresh look—perhaps in the originative pattern—at what they are doing.

Each demapattern has its own uses and dangers. To get the greatest benefit and to stay out of trouble, we should understand the demapatterns before we start wholesale transformations. Converting sales or engineering practices to strictly responsive rules could stultify those departments. Converting accounting and personnel practices to strictly goal-directed approaches could create chaos.

**The Vital Link**

We can talk about talk, draw maps of maps, and make decisions about decisions. Every medium we use to carry meanings appears to possess this peculiar self-reflexiveness, this recursive ability. Do not dismiss it as a mere logician's toy. Recursiveness really matters.

The linkage that identifies recursive demalogic is a decision about a decision.

**Table 10**      **The recursive demalinkage**

| Demalogic | Identifying Linkage |
|---|---|
| Recursive | decision about a decision |

Recursiveness works both forward and backward. For example, working forward, we can choose today to set March 15 as the date by which we will decide our summer plans. Working backward, we can now decide to overrule the decision we made last summer to stay home next summer.

Recursiveness works with any combination of demapatterns. We could, for example, adopt the goal of practicing originative demalogic. Or we could adopt the responsive rule of establishing three new short-term goals for each day.

We could decide to make only goal-directed weight-reduction eating decisions at home but to abandon them in favor of absolute and action-comparative, forget-the-consequences, eating decisions when on vacation. Carrying this idea to one logical extreme, we could embrace the goal of developing a set of responsive rules to identify the situations in which it would be appropriate for us to use each different demalogic.

"I'VE CHANGED MY MIND—CAN WE GO TO A MOVIE INSTEAD?"

Recursiveness also works with all the other demalinkages. We could, for example, decide to standardize all company directives by recasting them in the responsive pattern. That would amount to a decision to change other decisions (recursive linkage) from their various present patterns into the responsive pattern (transformative linkage). In similar manner we can combine recursiveness easily with each of the demalinkages yet to be introduced.

When we reach demasystems, level 6 on our scale of demastructures, we will again address this matter of recursive demalogic. We will show how law and all demasystems depend on recursiveness. Its profound importance in all human affairs will then be clear. Indeed, we will see that without recursiveness the linked decisions on which our civilization depends would unhook and let our civilization come apart.

**The Unavoidable Link**

Nobody in the pub need regret the price of beer if—as in the *The Hitchhiker's Guide to the Galaxy*—the world is scheduled to end in ten minutes. The patrons might just as well spend their entire pay on beer. Under the circumstances, saving some for the rent has become pointless.

Matters are seldom so clear-cut, and that is where allocative demalogic creeps in. Allocative demalogic concerns the sometimes annoying effect that one action—say, downing another beer—could have on the *availability* of other actions—such as paying the rent or getting home on time.

### Table 11     The allocative demalinkage

| Demalogic | Identifying Linkage |
|---|---|
| Allocative | effect of one action on availability of another action |

Money allocations make good examples. However, our greatest use of allocative demalogic concerns an even more fundamental resource – time. For every decision we make regarding money, we must make dozens on how we will use our time. And time, unlike money, once gone, cannot be regained.

> Now, of my threescore years and ten,
> Twenty will not come again,
> And take from seventy springs a score,
> It only leaves me fifty more.
>   And since to look at things in bloom
> Fifty springs are little room,
> About the woodlands I will go
> To see the cherry hung with snow.
>   A. E. Housman, *A Shropshire Lad*

Allocating time differs in still another way from allocating money. We may know how much money we have in the bank, but none of us knows how much time we have left. Housman's "seventy springs" is just a poetic average. All we know for sure is that our time-account, actuarially set at about 25,000 days, is running relentlessly out. We cannot make our sun stand still.

> Had we but world enough, and time,
> This coyness, lady, were no crime. . .
> My vegetable love should grow
> Vaster than empires, and more slow;
> An hundred years should go to praise
> Thine eyes, and on thy forehead gaze;
> Two hundred to adore each breast,
> But thirty thousand to the rest;. . .
> For, Lady, you deserve this state,
> Nor would I love at lower rate.
>   But at my back I always hear
> Time's wingèd chariot hurrying near. . .
>   Andrew Marvell, *To His Coy Mistress*

Most actions, on close scrutiny, appear simultaneously to increase the availability of some later actions while reducing the availability of others. For example, buying a car makes it easier to get around but reduces the money avail-

# The unavoidable link 53

able for redecorating.

Sometimes – and here allocative demalogic pays off big – the reduced availability later reverses. The car helps us make more money for redecorating.

Allocative demalogic has important uses. It permits us to budget our time, our money, and our other resources in the most efficient manner. By planning ahead, gauging how each action affects the next, we can reduce the waste from projects started but never finished and from projects gone stale while waiting for a subtask that should have been started earlier. We can select first the projects that return soonest the resources invested.

We employ allocative demalogic widely in business matters. Budgets allocate money. Sales programs budget time. Numerous on-the-spot decisions allocate materials. Entrepreneurs – and oil company executives generally – calculate the payout time of alternative investments.

We also use allocative demalogic at home in budgeting, planning our time, assigning storage space, and stretching ingredients for meals. We may tackle simple chores with fast payouts – for example, weatherstripping and plugging damaging leaks – before taking on longer-range projects. How much time and other resources we will have for other pursuits depends greatly on which ones we select first.

Could you help me find something good to read for an hour until my next train?

Like every other demalogic, allocative demalogic presents its own challenge and danger.

The challenge of allocative demalogic lies in learning to think in terms of chains of decisions interacting with limited resources. We find it easier to regard each decision as an isolated action. Some of our actions – like how we squandered our first good chunk of money or free time – later appear to us as allocatively naive. We simply weren't thinking about how one act affects another, but just of what appealed to us for itself at the moment.

We tend to regard resources (time, money, etc.) as what we either do or do not have. Yet every decision affects our resources for the next decision. Indeed, when we work to develop our resources, unexpected new courses of action often occur. A Swiss chemist trying to develop a stainproof tablecloth created cellophane. Blaise Pascal experimented with perpetual motion and invented roulette.

**Table 12** **The basic demalinkages**

| Demalogic | Identifying Linkage |
|---|---|
| Transformative | conversion of a decision from one to another demapattern |
| Recursive | decision about a decision |
| Allocative | effect of one action on availability of another action |

Some people mistakenly identify allocative demalogic with scheduling. But allocative demalogic concerns the effect of one action on another, a deeper matter, as inveterate schedulers sometimes rudely discover.

The executive committee meets at 10:00; your son wants to see you at 10:15; your wife said to call your mother at 10:30; the grievance committee will be here at 10:40; you are to call your lawyer at 10:45; you have three interviews at 10:50, 10:55, and 11:00 for a new secretary; and your plane for L.A. leaves at 11:45 from Kennedy.

# The unavoidable link

Deciders good at allocative demalogic face the danger of coming to fancy the process for its own sake. Efficiency and the husbanding of resources start to crowd out other demalogics. The plan becomes more important than the product. Thrift becomes miserliness. Much else goes to waste in an effort to eliminate waste. For in the end, who cares how much we saved by arriving on a cheaper flight one day *after* the wedding?

---

**WHICH BASIC DEMALINKAGE WOULD YOU USE?**

If you could use the three basic demalinkages (transformative, recursive, and allocative) just twice each, which would you use for these six cases?
1. To pack a car trunk. ........................ _____
2. To justify a policy. ........................ _____
3. To assign responsibilities. ................. _____
4. To systematize a business operation that has grown unwieldy. ................................. _____
5. To develop a school's classroom schedule. ...... _____
6. To review the actions of subordinates. .......... _____

(Answers on last page of this installment)

---

[The example below applies several demapatterns described in our two previous installments (*Et cetera*, Spring and Summer, 1988). We have pulled its three sections together from different parts of the *Master Atlas* for this installment. Ed.]

## WHAT WOULD YOU DO?

We are in the factory conference room of the small nonunion plant of ABC Metal Stampings. Earlier today, a high-pressure air hose came loose from #3 press. The hose swung away violently, scattering a box of finished stampings in all directions. Fortunately, personal injuries were limited to minor cuts and bruises. Order has now been restored on the factory floor, and the plant manager has called a meeting of his executive committee.

The members of the committee besides the plant manager (PLANT) are the production manager (PROD), the personnel director (PERS), the comptroller (COMPT), and the research director (RES). *Try to catch the demapatterns used by each participant.*

PLANT: What happened to #3 press?

PROD: A loose fitting was reported yesterday, and Joe was told to fix it, but he didn't, and so we had the accident. We should get rid of him.

PERS: Joe's had a good record. He shouldn't be punished for one error.

COMPT: It's too bad it happened, but what we need to make sure of is that it doesn't happen again.

PROD: Oh, let's not just pass some more accident-prevention regulations. The trouble is Joe. He's undependable and insubordinate, and as long as we depend on him we'll have trouble.

RES: What would happen if we just forgot it happened?

PERS: That's what I say. Look at all the trouble we'll have if we fire Joe. His whole section will be up in arms.

PROD: We can't let that keep us from doing what's *right*. Joe's guilty. He's got to pay somehow. We do agree he's guilty?

COMPT: I don't think there's any doubt that Joe made a mistake which caused the accident. But the real answer to this problem is not whatever we do to Joe—it's what we do to cut down on accidents. That's what will help the business.

PERS: Right. The business and cutting down on accidents are what's really important.

RES: How about using Joe to lead off an accident prevention program?

PLANT: It's a bad time for all this. I wish it had never happened. I can't get into it further now. We'll take it up again Tuesday.

To break the impasse that is building in the executive committee, a good first step is to peg the demapatterns being used by each member. Therefore, how would you describe the demalogic of the plant manager? Of the production manager? Of the personnel director? Of the comptroller? Of the research director?

(Answers on next page)

Conference room

## ANSWERS TO "WHAT WOULD YOU DO?" ON PREVIOUS PAGE

The executive committee members have revealed the following about their demalogics.
1. The plant manager has left the door open for someone to develop a plan before next Tuesday but has given no indications of what demalogic to use. (People don't usually get to be plant managers by trying to do everything themselves.)
2. The production manager is using a responsive demamap. ("Joe's guilty." "We should get rid of him.") The production manager's emphasis is on defining the situation ("Joe was told to fix it, but he didn't...") and finding an appropriate response ("He's got to pay somehow").
3. The personnel director jumps from one demamap to another, adopting any reasons that protect Joe. First comes a responsive argument ("Joe's had a good record..."), then what appears to be a scorecard objection ("Look at all the trouble we'll have if we fire Joe"), and finally some goals ("The business and cutting down on accidents are what is really important").
4. The comptroller has a consistently goal-directed demamap. Seeing that this particular accident "doesn't happen again" is an immediate goal that would serve the larger goal "to cut down on accidents," which in turn would serve the still larger goal to "help the business." The comptroller attempts to mollify the production manager ("Joe made a mistake"), but defines the "problem" not as Joe but as "accidents."
5. The research director has asked two open-ended questions about unjudged alternaquences ("What would happen if we just forgot it happened?" and "How about using Joe to lead off an accident prevention program?"). They reveal an originative demamap.

★ ★ ★ ★ ★

So, what have we? A plant manager who wants someone else to handle the matter. A production manager who wants to make Joe pay somehow. A personnel director who wants to protect Joe. A comptroller who wants to cut down on accidents. A research director who wants to explore alternaquences first and make a judgment later.

## HOW WOULD YOU SELL THE OTHERS?

Now, here's the payoff question. If you were the research director, how would you approach each of the other executive committee members and Joe to get approval for the plan you expressed last at the meeting of using Joe to lead off an accident prevention program?

(Answers on next page)

> **ANSWERS TO "HOW WOULD YOU SELL THE OTHERS?" ON PREVIOUS PAGE**
>
> Here's a plan for resolving the impasse that has come out of the first meeting.
>
> 1. Advise the plant manager that you have an idea that might bring everyone together and that you'd like to take a whack at it unofficially, unless there is some objection. (You should expect to obtain an unofficial blessing. If asked, you should beg off answering questions at this point about what you have in mind, to retain freedom to maneuver.)
> 2. Then, go to the production manager. Start by making the point that you have not yet seen the personnel director or the comptroller. In the language of the responsive pattern, agree that "Joe is guilty and should pay somehow." Show the production manager that you understand these responsive feelings. Then propose as "Joe's payment for his error" that Joe should lead off an accident prevention program. This would expose Joe's error to everyone (and, not incidentally, get Joe out from under the production manager for a while). Joe's role in the accident prevention program would be to call attention to the problem with #3 press and his involvement in it. (Expect to convince the production manager that this sequence of events is the most fitting you can think of for Joe's error.)
> 3. Go next to the personnel director to determine whether there would be any adverse repercussions from having Joe lead off an accident prevention program. (Expect to find none and to enlist the support of the personnel director in selling this new, temporary, and heroic role to Joe.)
> 4. After speaking to Joe, possibly with the personnel director in attendance, present your plan to the comptroller. (Expect no difficulty; for your plan will serve the comptroller's goal of cutting accidents and helping the business.)
> 5. Finally, return to the plant manager to announce what has been accomplished. Ask the plant manager to convene the executive committee immediately to confirm the arrangement. Then use the various demalogics quickly in turn to explain the situation, the proposed appropriate action, and the goals it would serve. Use tactful demalogical words to show each person that you understand his or her point of view. Keep it brief. (Expect all to ratify the decision. If you don't expect this outcome, don't propose the meeting to the plant manager at this time.)

Some people might feel it hypocritical to vary one's demalogic to match that of each decider one wishes to persuade. They would prefer either one demamap or open agreement that we have more than one demamap. Of course, it would be hypocritical if the research director couldn't honestly call up the feelings associated with the limited demamaps being used by the production manager and the comptroller. But able demalogicians handle limited demamaps in stride. They can, for example, simultaneously lament lost innocence and welcome new insights. That point aside, why delay agreement until everyone masters comparative demalogics?

[To be continued. In the next installment: the final decision-making linkages in the *Master Atlas*, the basic human link, two more human links, the *extra-human* links, the web that binds us all, and a foreword on how and where time-binding fits.]

### ANSWERS TO THE QUESTIONS EARLIER, ON PAGE 46

The answers most people give (there are no certainly right or wrong answers) are:
1. Responsive (if the telephone rings, answer it)
2. Action-comparative (pick whichever seat you prefer, nothing else is involved)
3. Goal-directed (get the child out fast, any way you can)
4. Originative (anticipate how alternaquences based on acceptance, refusal, negotiation, etc., would work out)
5. Absolute (based on the first helping and how you now feel)
6. Scorecard (weigh the advantages and disadvantages of taking the new place)

### ANSWERS TO THE QUESTIONS ON BASIC DEMALINKAGES

The usual answers are:
1. Allocative (each item packed affects the kind of space left for the other items)
2. Transformative (what kinds of reasons best support the policy?)
3. Recursive (decide what each person will have to decide)
4. Transformative (reduce the operation as much as possible to responsive rules)
5. Allocative (assign classes, teachers, and rooms, so that all fit)
6. Recursive (decide what action, if any, to take regarding the subordinates' decisions)

*Commentary six*

[EDITOR'S FOREWORD: Alfred Korzybski's 1921 book, with the now problematic title *Manhood of Humanity*, distinguished between animals as space-binders and human beings as time-binders characterized "by the power to make the past live in the present and the present for the future" (p. 67).

> There can be no doubt that humanity belongs to a class of life which to a large extent determines its own destinies, establishes its own rules of education and conduct, and thus influences every step we are free to take within the structure of our social system. But the power of human beings to determine their own destinies is limited by natural law, Nature's law. It is the counsel of wisdom to discover the laws of nature, including the laws of human nature, and then to live in accordance with them. The opposite is folly. (p. 5)

Korzybski's efforts to discover the nature of human time-binding led to general semantics (*Science and Sanity*, p. 8). How fitting then that MacNeal, whose theories extend general semantics, should call the propositional linkage between decisions "the basic human link." Our ability to send proposals to unknown other ahead and to respond anew to past proposals lies at the heart of time-binding. A dog can beg for a favor here and now but only a human can, for example, leave a will.

To have effect, however, a will depends on other decisional linkages, especially the recursive and organizational linkages. Each linkage has risen high from its biological roots through language, on which our decision-making systems now depend (MacNeal, *Demalogics*, propositions 12-12.8). Thus, language, time-binding, and civilization itself are woven into the fabric of this *Master Atlas of Decision Making*.

Here is a synopsis of the first five installments (*Et cetera*, Fall 1987 through Fall 1988):

In making decisions we use various demamaps (*decision-making maps*) that are not the decision-making territory, do not represent all the territory, and have working structures (demalogics) showing the decider's perspective. Examples are weighing the pros and cons, selecting fitting actions, pursuing goals, and previewing alternative futures.

Once past our favorite rationalizations, we find seven levels of demalogical structure: level (1) *subdecisional events*, (2) *basic demapatterns* [one action for one reason], (3) *compound demapatterns* [one action for multiple reasons], (4) *basic linkages* between decisions [which one decider can make], (5) *interpersonal linkages*, (6) self-reinforcing *systems* of interpersonal decisions, and (7) *comparative demalogics*.

Subdecisional events (level 1) include *situations* (what we can't change) and *alternaquences* (what we can do or influence, from *altern*ative and *conse*-*quences*). Verbally splitting "actions" from "consequences" induces a presumptuous elementalism; for we cannot have our actions without their consequences.

All basic demapatterns (level 2) except the originative exhibit this elementalism. So does the scorecard pattern at level 3.

| Demapattern | Formula |
|---|---|
| absolute | If you like action x, do x. |
| action-comparative | If you prefer action x to action y, do x. |
| responsive | If situation x occurs, do action y. |
| goal-directed | To get goal x, do action y. |
| originative | If you prefer alternaquence x to alternaquence y, do x. |
| scorecard | If x's good points outweigh its bad points, or if x's net score beats y's net score, do x. |

We ordinarily use the first two patterns for simpler personal matters, underestimate our reliance on the responsive, overestimate our use of the goal-directed, and by adhering to elementalistic "values" skip over the originative pattern to the scorecard.

Each pattern has its own uses and dangers. Some patterns allow consequences to be ignored. Some hamper coordination.

Any action we choose in one pattern we could also choose in any other pattern. Pattern shifts (in choice or later explanations) form the *transformative linkage*, a *basic linkage* at level 4. Two other basic linkages can be used by a solitary decider: the vital *recursive linkage* (decisions about decisions), and the almost always applicable *allocative linkage* (the effect one action has on the *availability* of other actions).

We now proceed to the structures at levels 5 and 6, the remaining decisional linkages...]

# 6. More logics for interconnected decisions

**The Basic Human Link**

All of the demalogics—both patterns and linkages—described to this point could be used by one person alone. Those that follow in the next few pages are interpersonal demalogics. They link at least two persons or—as we will see in the case of organizational demalinkages—two demaunits. (In terms of the levels shown on [table 1 in the second installment], we now move to level 5.)

Interpersonal demalogic would stall at the start if we could not suggest courses of action to each other. However, through word and gesture we do almost continually propose actions to others and they to us. The courses of action so proposed identify the most fundamental interpersonal demalogic, the propositional demalinkage.

We propose courses of action to each other in many different styles. Because these styles reflect the relative demastatus of the proposers and deciders—a matter of interest to us—our language has given the different styles distinctive names. Appeals, bids, claims, commands, demands, directives, offers, orders, petitions, requests, rules, suggestions, warnings, and the like, however, all have the propositional linkage in common. They are in that sense, all of them, proposals.

Sometimes people say that they have no choice except to follow an order, especially one backed up by threats. But that overstates the case, doesn't it? Even the most coercive proposals—"Your money or your life"—are still proposals, because some choice, no matter how poor or burdened with unsought circumstances, still remains with the persons to whom the actions are proposed. We can certainly distinguish these cases from those truly offering no choice, where, for example, victims are killed without notice and *then* robbed.

**Table 13      The propositional demalinkage**

| Demalogic | Identifying Linkage |
|---|---|
| Propositional | course of action proposed by one person to another |

The demalogics others employ in their proposals may give important clues on where they're coming from. By catching the clues, we boost our chances of talking their language.

A bare recitation of alternatives ("oil and vinegar, French, or Italian") generally signals that we are free to do what we like in the absolute pattern.

An insistence on defining the situation (for example, "Are they guilty or innocent?") or finding fitting actions ("What would be right?") discloses the responsive pattern.

An emphasis on objectives ("What should we be trying to achieve?") or means ("How do we do it?") clearly marks the goal-directed pattern.

A suggestion to preview alternaquences ("Think through what your life would be like both ways") may indicate the originative pattern.

A reference to pros and cons, drawbacks, or bottom lines reveals the scorecard pattern.

As participants in propositional demalinkages—whether as proposers or deciders—we can gain from reasoning with people in their own terms. These are the demalogics to which they are most receptive.

**Two More Human Links—#1: Mutual**

Few would expect conflict, competition, and cooperation—as dissimilar as war and peace—to share a common demalogical characteristic. Yet each depends on two or more deciders' selecting a like action. The action may be a feud, a footrace, or an operatic duet. No matter, it takes at least two participants. What if they gave a war and only one person came?

Whenever the course of action in our decision requires a like action by another decider, we find ourselves needing a mutual demalinkage.

# Two more human links—#1 mutual

**Table 14**  **The mutual demalinkage**

| Demalogic | Identifying Linkage |
|---|---|
| Mutual | like actions by deciders that none could take alone |

We may then turn to mutual demamaps. "Do you want to fight? Race? Make love? How about a game of chess? Would you help me move this table." Our proposed course of action depends on a partner's joining in the action.

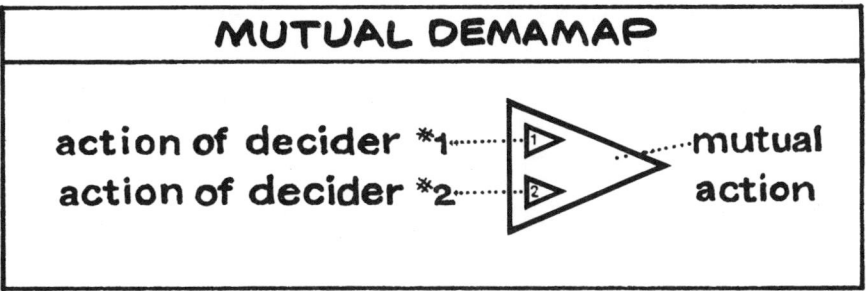

However, nothing requires our partner to join in the reasons we may have for that action.

— **#2: Reciprocal**
Mutual demalogic grades subtly into reciprocal demalogic, where we act in exchange for a dissimilar action from someone else.

**Table 15**      **The reciprocal demalinkage**

| Demalogic | Identifying Linkage |
|---|---|
| Reciprocal | unlike actions that deciders take in exchange |

Such exchanges can be as routine as commuters buying newspapers or as singular and complex as corporations merging. Every reciprocal demalinkage, however, presumes that the deciders will be bound by the responsive rule, "If you do what you have agreed (or is expected), I'll do what I've agreed (or is expected)." This makes a reciprocal demamap look very different from a mutual demamap.

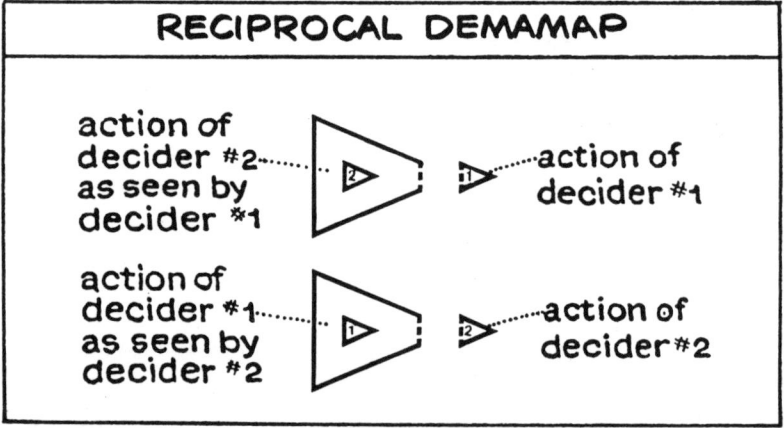

One thing that doesn't change between mutual and reciprocal demalinkages is the principle of demapattern freedom. We need to agree on the reciprocal actions, but our reasons can remain our own. We can buy a house *to get more room* from owners who are selling *because of an out-of-state job transfer.*

Obvious as the principle of demapattern freedom appears, it is neither intuitive nor inborn. If it were, we wouldn't need parental warnings to refuse candy from strangers. Nor would we be surprised to discover that our partners in decision, perhaps with whom we have had many successful mutual and reciprocal demalinkages, may all along have had reasons for their participation in a demalogic different from ours.

### The Extrahuman Links

Anyone who joins an organized group soon discovers that the organization in some sense has a life of its own. It ages. It interacts with humans and with other organizations. It issues proposals and decisions in its own name. It begets other organizations. It can perish. The organization has a demalife.

We must deal, then, with two species of demalife, human and organizational. Both make decisions, but how different the species are!

The extrahuman links

**Table 16  Demaspecies comparisons**

| Aspect Compared | Species of Demaunit ||
|---|---|---|
| | Person | Organization |
| Source | two parents | one to many demaunits |
| Demaunit | person | organization (firm, church, congress, office, committee, cartel, club, etc.) |
| Beginning | birth following conception | formation following agreement, directive, etc. |
| Dematraining period | 18+ years | none necessarily |
| Interspecies propagation | yes, people can create organizations | no, organizations do not create people |
| Agent | self, usually | officials, usually |
| Staffing | does not apply | appointment, hiring, election, coup, etc. |
| Initial "policy" source | heredity and training | charter and custom |
| Life span | 70+ years | 1,000+ years |
| End | death or incompetence | dissolution, merger, dismissal, etc. |

All organizational demalogic involves at least one of four kinds of linkage with an extrahuman demaunit.

First comes enfounding demalogic, identified by action founding (or dissolving) an extrahuman demaunit. The demaunit might be a club, a team, a committee, a firm, a government, or even a single official position, provided that the demaunit has its own demacapabilities. The founders usually supply these capabilities in the form of initial resources and policies.

Second comes enstaffing demalogic. The organization needs people to animate its demafunctions. The action identifying enstaffing demalogic can be an election, appointment, inheritance, purchase, even a coup; or in reverse, firings, disbandings, even annihilation.

Third comes functionarial demalogic. The organization's staff are expected to perform not as individual private deciders but as functionaries, as members and officials of the organization. Such official or company actions identify functionarial demalogic.

Having come this far, the organization now possesses a fourth demalogic, the ability to use for itself the first two organizational demalogics (enfounding and enstaffing) used initially by persons. Through this second-order organizational demalogic, companies form trade associations and countries appoint ambassadors to represent them at the United Nations.

**Table 17**  **The organizational demalinkages**

| Demalogic | Identifying Linkage |
|---|---|
| Enfounding | action founding or terminating an extrahuman demaunit |
| Enstaffing | action staffing or destaffing an extrahuman demaunit |
| Functionarial | action by the staff animating an extrahuman demaunit |
| Second-order | functionarial enfounding or enstaffing a further demaunit |

Each of these four demalogics links actions and deciders in a distinct manner. Yet, if we wish to overlook the distinctions, we may refer to all four as the organizational demalinkage.

**Table 18**  **The organizational demalinkage**

| Demalogic | Identifying Linkage |
|---|---|
| Organizational | action founding, staffing, or animating extrahuman demaunit |

Some texts treat organizational decisions as if they were models for all decisions. Yet the behavior of one species can hardly be the best model for a different species with a different life span and filling a different demalogical niche.

Take pleasures, for example. No organizational decision is like deciding to have a lemonade. Organizations don't make absolute, action-comparative, or originative decisions based simply on what *they* like, dislike, or prefer. Decisions that appear to be of this kind turn out (1) either to be reducible to organizational standards (rules and goals) or (2) to be personal choices (sometimes allowable within the organization, and sometimes not).

Even though we act in both capacities, we can usually separate our personal from our functionarial decisions. We may personally thank others for our election and then hear ourselves in the next breath issue our first official pronouncement.

# The extrahuman links

A single company can contain many further demaunits, such as departments and committees. Each department or committee in turn may include a chief and many other functionaries. Thus, there are more functionaries than demaunits and more demaunits than companies. The same holds true for clubs, governments, and other kinds of organizations.

We can distinguish and obtain fairly accurate counts of four major kinds of whole organizations: businesses, families, governments, and all others (primarily churches, clubs, and schools). But who knows how many business committees there are or how many members they have? For this and similar reasons we can estimate only roughly the numbers of demaunits and functionaries. Here are my current guesstimates for the United States.

**Table 19        Demaunits and functionaries**

| Type of Organization | Estimated Millions of | | |
| --- | --- | --- | --- |
| | Organizations* | Demaunits | Functionaries |
| Business | 16.5 | 170 | 300 |
| Family | 65.0 | 230 | 400 |
| Government | .1 | 2 | 400 |
| Other** | 1.2 | 15 | 200 |
| Total | 82.8 | 417 | 1,300 |
| * whole organizations as usually counted.<br>**primarily churches, clubs, and schools. | | | |

Since only about 250 million people live today in the United States, each of us on average must serve as more than five functionaries to meet the 1,300 million total. For most adults that would probably include duties (as voters, taxpayers, residents, jurors, etc.) in two governmental demaunits. For couples with minor children, each adult would function both as spouse and as parent. That's already four functionarial positions. Young children and prison inmates would have fewer. Readers of this *Master Atlas* would typically have many more. How many functionaries are you now? 10? 30? 100? How many have you *ever* been? 100? 300? 1,000?

# The extrahuman links

Apart from the direct demalogics (absolute, action-comparative, and originative), the official decisions of organizations use all the demalogics used by individuals. Organizations continually employ responsive and goal-directed demapatterns, and use the compound patterns and all the demalinkages.

However, by dividing themselves into departments, organizations permit demalogical specialization. Because of this specialization, the sales and law departments of one corporation resemble each other less than they resemble their counterparts in other corporations. To find our way around an organization, to understand how its many decisions are being made, we must pay attention to this demalogical specialization.

**Table 20**         **Demalogical emphasis**

| Place or Role | Responsive | Goal-directed | Transformative | Allocative | Propositional | Reciprocal | Organizational |
|---|---|---|---|---|---|---|---|
| Bureaucracy | x | | | | | | |
| Citizen | x | | | | | | |
| Police | x | x | | | | | |
| Production | x | x | | | | | |
| Law court | x | | x | | | | |
| School | x | x | | x | | | |
| Engineer | x | x | | x | | | |
| Spouse | x | x | | | | x | |
| Minister | x | x | x | | x | | |
| Supervisor | x | x | | x | x | | |
| Parent | x | x | x | x | x | | |
| Labor union | x | x | x | | | x | x |
| Legislature | x | x | x | x | x | x | x |
| Advertising & sales | | x | x | x | x | | |
| Entrepreneur | | x | | x | | x | x |
| Top management | | x | x | x | x | x | x |

Most organizational functions emphasize both the responsive and goal-directed patterns; all use one or the other. Thus, the benefits of these patterns (coordination and purposefulness) and their dangers (ignored consequences and avoidance of responsibility) are compounded in organizational decisions.

Note how experience in one function – even in the short list above – can prepare or fail to prepare its animator for another function. For example, almost any bureaucrat would understand how to be a citizen. An engineer would be three-fourths prepared (three out of four demalogics) to be a production supervisor.

On the other hand, one's familiarity as a judge with transformative demalogic would not help one to be an engineer.

In some cases a reliance on one demalogic (as on responsive demalogic by bureaucrats) might hinder functionarial efforts elsewhere (in advertising, for example).

The chart on demalogical emphasis also provides one reason why retirement from organizational functions creates difficulties. How does one exercise one's well-honed organizational demalogics by going fishing or watching TV?

---

**CAN YOU MATCH THE DEMALINKAGES?**

Find the numbered example that best illustrates each lettered demalinkage.

| basic | interpersonal | organizational |
|---|---|---|
| a. transformative | d. propositional | g. enfounding |
| b. recursive | e. mutual | h. enstaffing |
| c. allocative | f. reciprocal | i. functionarial |
|  |  | j. second-order |

1. Aaron Burr and Alexander Hamilton fought a pistol duel in 1804. ___
2. I'm going to take flying lessons ___
3. The first thing she did was form a corporation ___
4. He said he was too sick to go on. I took that to mean he no longer cared whether or not the show succeeded ___
5. [sign before a bridge] BRIDGE SURFACE FREEZES BEFORE ROADWAY ___
6. The five companies decided to form a trade association ___
7. She sold me her ticket for $40 ___
8. I've decided to make my choice by Thursday ___
9. The public relations officer said the company would have no comment at this time ___
10. I selected Tom to be the coach ___

(Answers on last page of this installment)

---

## The Web

Our ancestors long ago discovered the sixth level of demastructure. By combining demalogics in a certain way, they created continually self-reinforcing networks of decisions—in short, demasystems.

Here is the secret of building demasystems. (1) Start with a responsive rule (for example, "Babies must be cared for") and make it functionarial ("by their parents"). (2) Use recursive demalogic to create a new responsive rule about observance of the first rule ("or corrective action should be taken") and make this rule functionarial ("by the Health Commissioner"). (3) Add further recursive, functionarial, responsive rules ("who may be removed by the Mayor, who may be recalled by the people") as needed.

Such recursive rules, especially when linking organizations perpetuated under still other, separate rules (like cities and families), identify demasystems.

# The web

**Table 21**      **The demasystems demalinkage**

| Demalogic | Identifying Demalinkage |
|---|---|
| Demasystem | responsive functionarial decision about responsive functionarial decision |

The greatest flowering of systems demalogic arises in the law. Indeed, to create law, rather than just a loose system like etiquette, one *must* work painstakingly with recursive demalogic. In the words of noted jurist H. L. A. Hart in his celebrated *The Concept of Law*:

> ... law may most illuminatingly be characterized as a union of primary rules ... with secondary rules ... about such rules ... supplemented by a description of the ... relationship of the officials ... to the ... rules which concern them as officials.

Law gives us whole tiers of official responsive decisions about other decisions. The first tier consists of responsive decisions following *primary* rules, defined as all those rules governing behavior other than rules about rules. The other tiers consist of responsive decisions following *secondary* rules of several kinds, but all are rules about rules (for example, rules about how rules are changed, delegated, recognized, adjudicated, and enforced). Consider, for example, the differences between a speed limit (a rule), a speeding ticket (pursuant to a rule about a broken rule), and a traffic court (more rules about the other rules, including rules triggered by how well the ticketing officer may have followed the rules).

> **ANSWERS TO THE QUESTIONS ON DEMALINKAGES**
> 1. e, mutual (neither could duel alone)
> 2. c, allocative (lessons make new actions available)
> 3. g, enfounding (founding an extrahuman demaunit)
> 4. a, transformative (converts responsive "too sick" to goal-directed judgment "no longer cared whether or not the show succeeded")
> 5. d, propositional (advice to drive carefully)
> 6. j, second-order (organizations founding an organization)
> 7. f, reciprocal (exchange of unlike actions)
> 8. b, recursive (decision about a decision)
> 9. i, functionarial (staff action animating an organization)
> 10. h, enstaffing (action filling an organizational position)

Such doubly-responsive recursive linkages serve as the backbone of all formal demasystems. Whether in settling questions of business law, church canon, or putting green protocol, we depend on responsive rules to advise us who is to determine what rules apply and who is to apply them.

Demasystems offer the great advantages of continuity and predictability. Capricious judgments can be reduced. Contracts can be enforced.

The chief danger of demasystems lies in their emphasis on functionarial responsive decisions, the hallmark of bureaucracy. Some relief can be obtained by building goals and allocative demalogic into the responsive rules. ("It is the duty of the sales manager to increase sales efficiency.") However, such efforts lead to the familiar conflict of goals with rules and fail to promote a general view of alternaquences.\*

This narrowness of view threatens us most when demasystems conflict. Our practice of embedding goals in self-reinforcing responsive systems helps explain how the otherwise reasonable functionaries of different religious, political, and economic systems could on occasion slaughter each other so gloriously in the name of all they hold good and true. [To be continued. In the next installment: views from the summit of comparative demalogics about error, forecasting, and demaconsciousness, plus a general trail map for determining which demalogics to apply in any given situation.]

---

\*Perhaps some relief could be gotten from rules encouraging originative demalogic, but today they must be rare.

*Commentary seven*

[EDITOR'S FOREWORD: I was reading recently an article on mindlessness and script theory.† A "script," it said, predisposes but doesn't require mindlessness, and "is a cognitive structure that specifies a typical sequence of occurrences in a given situation." By page two I was wondering how such scripts and "mindlessness" related to the responsive pattern, which fashions decisions in the form, "if x occurs, do y." The characteristics of behaviors following scripts and the responsive pattern (see the third installment of this series) match that well.

Next I found myself wondering whether a thoroughgoing demalogical approach wouldn't be the easier and more explicit one. It would show how the responsive pattern can simplify decisions and lead to "mindlessness," how coupling the pattern with organizational linkages can produce bureaucracies, and yet how combining it with the transformative and recursive linkages can stimulate the deepest type of legal thoughtfulness (see our previous installment). Two difficulties with script theory would be reduced; for the responsive pattern can be identified through speech (see the factory accident example in our fifth installment) and its antidotes are already known (see "Error" in this installment).

If such a bridge of psychology, organization theory, law, and linguistics can be built on the responsive pattern, what might we expect from a thoroughgoing demalogical approach also using the absolute pattern, the goal-directed, the originative, the scorecard, the propositional linkage, the reciprocal, the allocative, and all the rest of our seven levels of demalogical structure?

---

†Blake E. Ashforth and Yitzhak Fried, "The Mindlessness of Organizational Behaviors," *Human Relations*, 1988, 4, 305-329.

And then I found myself with a new question and previewing a wondrous alternaquence. Could it be that the social sciences differ from natural science and each other exactly in these demalogical considerations and that the *Master Atlas* will permit us to relate them all to one grand scheme, to pool our energies for a vast breakout of knowledge? Like Kilroy, silently witnessing our deeds from the height of comparative demalogics, for that moment I was there.

Here is a highly condensed synopsis of the first six installments (*Et cetera,* Fall 1987 through Winter 1988):

We use various demamaps (*de*cision-*ma*king *maps*) with working structures (demalogics) on seven levels: (1) *subdecisional events,* (2) *basic demapatterns* [one action for one reason], (3) *compound demapatterns* [one action for multiple reasons], (4) *basic linkages* between decisions [makeable by one decider], (5) *interpersonal linkages,* (6) self-reinforcing *systems* of interpersonal decisions, and (7) *comparative demalogics.*

Subdecisional events (level 1) include *situations* (what we can't change) and *alternaquences* (what we can do or influence, from *alterna*tive and conse*quences*). Verbally splitting "actions" from "consequences" induces a presumptuous elementalism; we cannot have one without the other. All basic demapatterns (level 2) except the originative exhibit this elementalism. So does the scorecard pattern at level 3.

| Demapattern | Formula |
| --- | --- |
| absolute | If you like action x, do x. |
| action-comparative | If you prefer action x to action y, do x. |
| responsive | If situation x occurs, do action y. |
| goal-directed | To get goal x, do action y. |
| originative | If you prefer alternaquence x to alternaquence y, do x. |
| scorecard | If x's good points outweigh its bad points, or if x's net score beats y's net score, do x. |

We ordinarily use the first two patterns for simpler personal matters, underestimate reliance on the responsive, overestimate use of the goal-directed, and by using elementalistic "values" skip over the originative pattern to the scorecard. Each pattern has its own uses and dangers.

The *basic linkages* (level 4) include the *transformative* (pattern shifts), the *recursive* (decisions about decisions), and the *allocative* (the effect one action has on the availability of other actions). The *interpersonal linkages* (level 5) include the *propositional* (actions proposed to other persons), the *mutual* (alike actions by deciders that none could take alone), the *reciprocal* (unlike actions that deciders take in exchange), and the *organizational* (actions founding, staffing, or animating extrahuman demaunits).

We now proceed to level 7, that of comparative demalogics, to see how things look when no one demalogic restricts our view. . .]

# 7. Applying demalogics

Welcome to level 7. We have now reached Kilroy's position [on page 17 in the second installment].

**Overview**
Time for a breather. Let's look around.
How many demalogics have we covered? The sections on logics for the single decision presented nine demapatterns (counting the three compounds defined in a footnote). The sections on logics for interconnected decisions presented eleven demalinkages (counting the organizational ones as four). That makes twenty demalogics.
If that seems like a lot, please note:
1. Excluding quantitative demalinkages, that's it; just twenty or so demalogics in all. There are no others.

A HORDE OF DECISIONS STORMS THE DEMALOGICAL REDOUBT

2. The twenty demalogics make most decisions so easy for us that we notice neither the decision nor our demalogic. Each of us uses demalogics perhaps one hundred million times in a lifespan, but we may be conscious of only one percent (one million) of those uses, and we would label still fewer as major decisions. What's twenty demalogics against that many uses?
3. If twenty demalogics seems a lot, might not that judgment stem from our understandable wish for simplicity and the discomfort we feel in the few decisions where demalogics clash?

Considering all the different kinds of decisions we face, we could more reasonably complain that twenty approaches isn't enough.

Anyway, most of us already knew that people approached decisions in different ways. It just didn't occur to us to think of *every* way as useful somewhere. We were probably either too busy seeking the best way for the decision at hand or defending the approach we had already settled on as generally the best.

Now we see, however, that each demalogic has its uses. We have an organized way to classify the demalogics and to list their best (and worst) uses. We have thereby put ourselves in a position to choose our demalogics consciously.

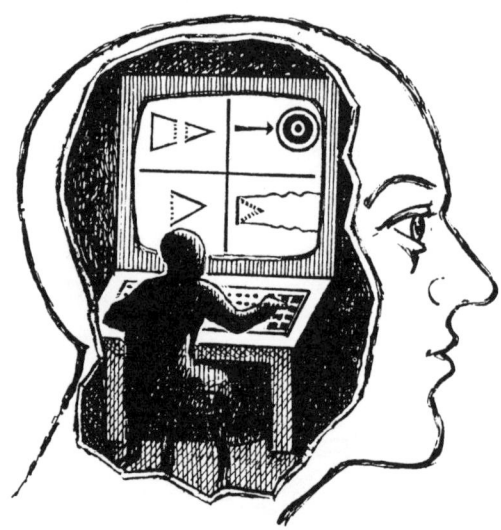

That's one thing comparative demalogics is about. Choosing the best demalogics for each new decision. Feeling free to choose. Knowing which approach makes the most sense in each case.

Selecting demalogics for decisions will be our next topic.

Beyond that, however, comparative demalogics also gives us valuable new ways to recognize and judge decisions, whether made by ourselves or others. Those topics will complete our grand tour.

## A Walk Through The Demagarden

When I first suggested that the *Master Atlas* needed at this point a one-page diagram simplifying demalogical selection my editors said it was a great idea, probably impossible given all the factors concerning twenty demalogics, but worth a try anyway. The outcome surprised us pleasantly. Because it looked like a garden maze [see overleaf], we called it "the demalogical selection walk," which soon became "demawalk" and often just "the walk."

The walk has thirty-eight numbered locations. Twenty-one, the rectangles, ask questions that guide one to different paths. Seventeen, the ovals, name the demalogics found on the paths. (Grouping three compound patterns at #36 and omitting the demasystem linkage, all of whose demalogical components do appear, accounts for the reduction from twenty.) The walk begins at the higher levels of decisional structure and proceeds to the lower levels. Thus, all the locations on paths in the top half (#1 through #20) cover demalinkages. The rest cover demapatterns.

The simplest path you can take through the walk runs directly down the left side (locations #1, #5, #11, #13, #21, #22, and #23). This would track a private decision, made entirely by you, not about another decision, not significantly affecting the availability of future actions, essentially about a matter of immediate personal taste with no significant consequences, in the form of a yes or no on a single choice. "Yes, I'll put pepper on my cucumber." The only oval on the path is #23. Absolute demalogic is all you need.

You would need more demalogics to function as a sales manager. In encouraging a recruit facing an unexpected turn, for example, your path might take you through the ovals at #2, #6, #14, and #16 until you reached the question at #26. There, by shunning "sales-at-any-cost" (which would lead straight to #35) in favor of "sales-within-the-rules," you might progress via #30 to #36. If so, you could use a commonplace business compound: the goal-directed pattern limited by the responsive pattern to actions consistent with company rules.

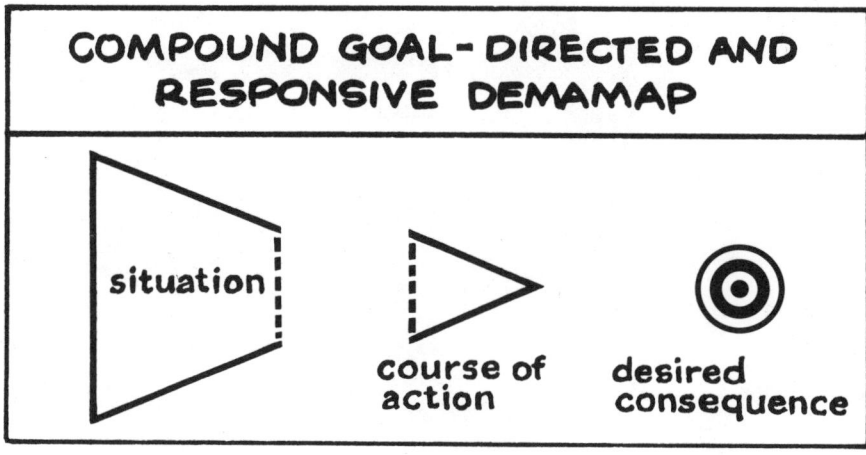

The demawalk does not explain how to use any demalogic, nor is that its intention. For most decisions the demawalk would be an unnecessary exercise, because deciders know without deliberation what demalogics to use and how to use them. Selecting demalogics in an organized way helps most in complicated decisions. Indeed, even knowing how demalogically complex a decision is can help, for then we can appreciate better what we are up against.

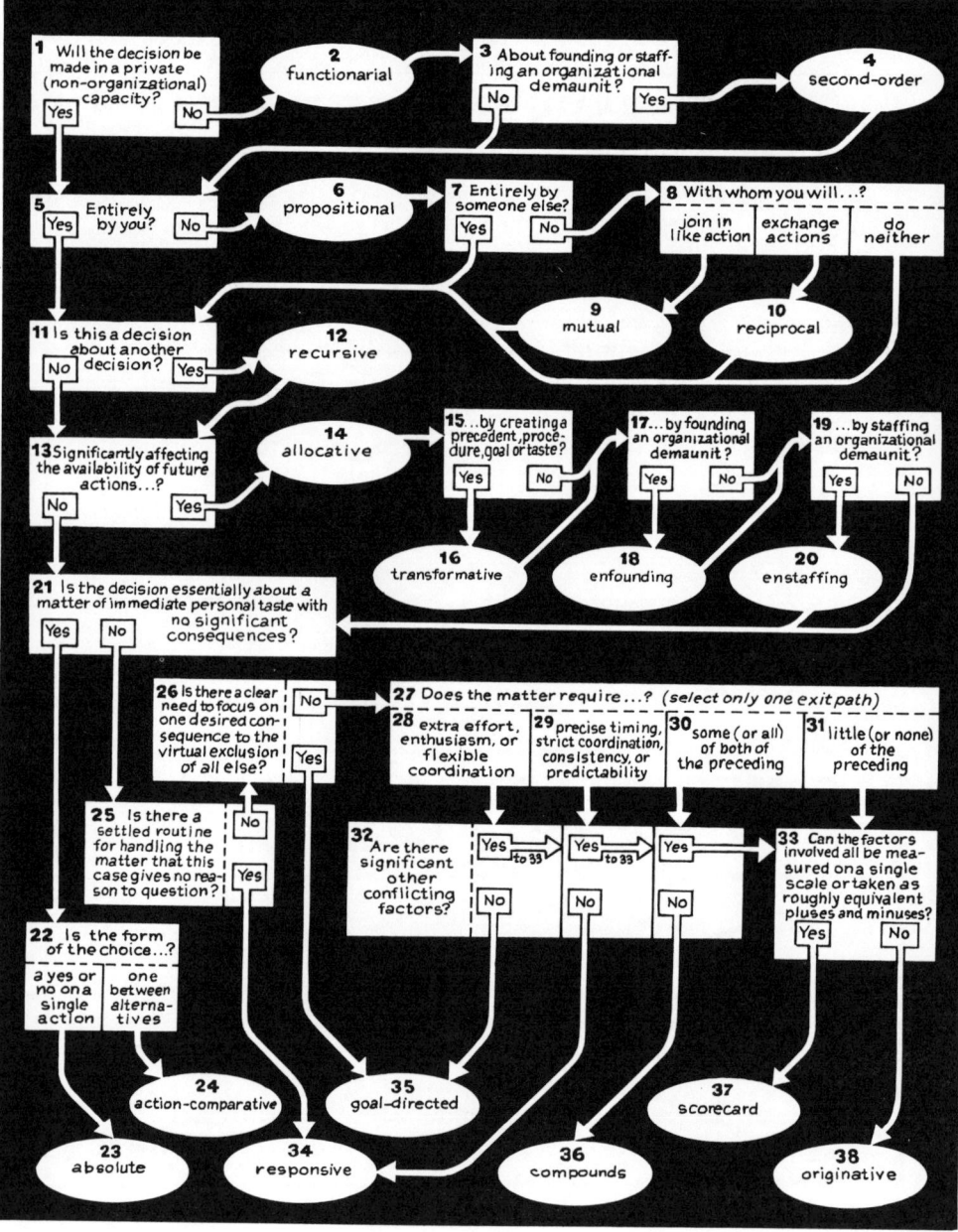

There are 4,050 different routes through the demalogical selection walk. Only a few of them are illogical (for example, a yes at #13 would seem to rule out a yes at #21). Some routes yield the same demalogics (for example, #25 to #34 directly or via #26, #27, #29, and #32). Nevertheless, if you walked through enough decisions, you could find about 1,000 different reasonable sets of demalogics. That means that learning just seventeen demalogics can prepare us for a thousand decisional paths. And as you might expect, the walk becomes much easier after the first few outings.

---

### WHICH PATH WOULD YOU TAKE?

Starting with location #1, list the numbered locations you would encounter on your path through the demalogical selection walk for these decisions:

1. You are in your kitchen alone and silently ask yourself whether you want a glass of water or tomato juice.
   1–_____

2. You are approaching a traffic light that has turned red.
   1–_____

3. You have received a non-negotiable offer of a three-year appointment to an office that interests you.
   1–_____

4. You are seriously considering a divorce.
   1–_____

5. As head of your corporation's public relations department, you are wondering whether, for the first time ever, to hire a back-up manager for the fall industrial show, just in case the present manager can't handle the load this year.
   1–_____

6. You are one of a panel of appellate judges reviewing a federal agency's novel decision.
   1–_____

(Answers on last page of this installment)

---

~~Erar~~  ~~Erer~~  ~~Erir~~  ~~Eror~~  ~~Erur~~  ~~Errer~~  ~~Errir~~
## Error

Error, like sex, is a staple of the comedian's repertoire. Perhaps part of the reason is that error, again like sex, is a pervasive but *taboo* natural phenomenon. Strict standards govern both the acceptability of error and of talk about error. Ignoring these standards exposes oneself to criticism and ridicule.

The scientific and academic communities haven't done much yet to classify and clarify error. The first Kinsey report on error has not yet appeared. Perhaps no one wants to cast the first stone.

Because each demalogic suffers from different kinds of possible error, comparative demalogics provides a new approach to this ticklish subject.

Comparative demalogics begins by dividing error into two major types: (1) errors of usage *within* (and visible from within) the demalogic being used, and (2) errors of oversight caused by (but visible only from *without*) the demalogic then being used.

Overdressing for a first date when you wanted so much to look just right falls into the first type of error. Given the goal-directed pattern, you can see that the means chosen don't achieve the end sought.

Forgetting your promise to visit a sick friend because of your preoccupation with preparing for the date would display the second type of error. By focusing your attention and efforts, the goal-directed pattern has pushed your promise into the shadow.

The two types of error turn up in different ways in different demalogics.

**Table 22      Errors in a four-demalogic world***

| Demalogic | Usage Errors Within the Demalogic | Overlooked per Three Other Demalogics |
|---|---|---|
| Absolute | 1. choosing thing not liked<br>2. not testing presumed dislike | 1. situations<br>2. alternatives<br>3. rules<br>4. goals<br>5. consequences (all)<br>6. option menu outcome |
| Responsive | 1. misclassifying situation<br>2. applying incorrect rule | 1. alternatives<br>2. likes and dislikes<br>3. goals<br>4. consequences (all)<br>5. option menu outcome |
| Goal-directed | 1. defining goal poorly<br>2. selecting wrong means | 1. situations<br>2. alternatives<br>3. likes and dislikes<br>4. rules<br>5. side effects<br>6. option menu outcome |
| Allocative | 1. misestimating effect of action chosen on the availability of other actions [the option menu outcome] | 1. situations<br>2. alternatives<br>3. likes and dislikes<br>4. rules<br>5. goals<br>6. consequences (some) |

*The lists in the last column would lengthen as more demalogics were added, because each would bring its own perspectives on error.

# Error

The demalogical specialization practiced by corporate departments reduces the type one errors of usage within the department. Accounting concentrates on the responsive pattern, classifying debits and credits so that financial reports can be produced in a consistent manner. Sales concentrates on the goal-directed and propositional demalogics, seeking ways to influence others to buy. Each department performs feats within its own demalogics that would baffle the other department.

However, this specialization fosters type two errors of oversight. These can lead to misunderstanding and conflict. High-powered salespeople easily resent being shackled by expense limits and the need to submit detailed supporting records. They want to pursue the sale, to scale new heights of innovative selling, to land the biggest order ever seen. Yet that seemingly fat contract that sales pursues may produce the largest accounting loss of the decade, a golden fleecing.

General managers know from experience about these differences. They expect each department to misunderstand the other's point of view. Bridging such demalogical gaps is part of general management's job.

Individual deciders can reduce their type one errors of usage within demalogics by (a) selecting the demalogics that best fit the circumstances and (b) acquiring more skill in the demalogics they use. Deciders can reduce their type two errors of oversight due to demalogical bias by (c) adding more demalogics to their repertoires and (d) remembering to vary their points of view to check matters from other perspectives.

Overreliance on a limited set of demalogics may produce obvious symptoms. For example:

**Table 23    Symptoms of demalogical overreliance**

| Demalogic | Symptoms |
|---|---|
| Absolute | overindulgence |
| Responsive | prejudice, feelings of righteousness or guilt, denial of responsibility |
| Goal-directed | toleration of unreasonable actions and effects, feelings of failure |
| Scorecard | internal conflict, excessive deliberation, cynical relativism |
| Allocative | stinginess, overfussy apportionment |

The general antidote in all such cases is an extended diet of other demalogics.

## Forecasting

Failure to forecast the overall effect of our actions heads the list of our errors. We need not search long for a reason. Except for the originative pattern, our demamaps don't even try to portray alternaquences. Hence we get little practice.

"I JUST TAKE THINGS AS THEY COME"

Yet every corner we turn, every conversation we hold, virtually every event in our lives provides an opportunity for forecasting and checking our forecasts. The intellectual exercise machines are there. All we need do is forecast the alternaquences, treat every truly unexpected event as a mapping error, and strive to improve. With an open mind, an easy fifty to sixty forecasts a day, and a pinch of probability theory, almost everyone's forecasting will improve rapidly.

For example, just before looking anything up in a reference book, just before you ask the price of anything—indeed, just before you get any question answered—*commit* yourself to a forecast of what you will find. The more you do it, the better you'll get. If you guessed a few hundred people's weights a day for one week, you too could work at the county fair.

Actually, the first and toughest hurdle in forecasting is the commitment. We all want to hedge, to say we really don't know, because we are so concerned about being right or wrong. So, out of fear of error, we avoid learning to fore-

# Forecasting

cast even simple events, let alone the overall effect of our actions. We kid ourselves that forecasting requires special knowledge, whereas what it requires most is practice.

Nobody can predict the future surely. An alternaquence, by definition, includes repercussions beyond our control. Perfect maps, like perfect athletic performances, rarely occur. But lack of practice doesn't help. Going entirely by the responsive book or by absolute likes and dislikes doesn't help. Focusing on goals helps no more than chaining a lookout to a fixed telescope. A scorecard map just adds more scopes. Only the originative pattern tries to forecast whole alternaquences.

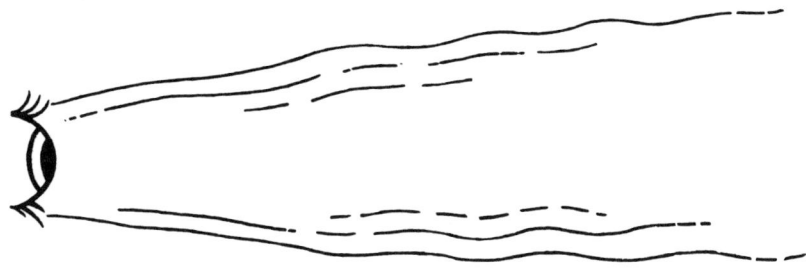

Originative demalogic provides practice in previewing alternaquences before judgment. Saving originative demalogic only for life's critical decisions—as many do—guarantees that we arrive at those junctures untrained.

### NONJUDGMENTAL FORECASTS

The U.S. National Weather Service forecasts weather independently of who might gain or lose from any particular forecast. Gradually since 1870, almost unnoticed, and without any power to control the weather, the Service has extended the range, reliability, and utility of its still questionable forecasts, which we remain free to use or ignore.

What if we applied the same approach to forecasting social alternaquences—say of major pending legislation—that are today as indeterminate as weather was in 1870? That is, what if we funded a national agency to forecast legislative alternaquences independently of which social programs might gain or lose from any particular forecast, and gave the agency no objective other than to extend the reliability, range, and timeliness of its forecasts, which we all remained free to use or ignore?

Might not the utility of such forecasts improve greatly over the next century?

## Demaconsciousness

If we take some people at their word, they never decide anything. I don't buy that. I define every acceptance-or-rejection-of-an-action-to-be-taken as a decision, whether conscious or unconscious, as long as it is not hopelessly beyond the reach of consciousness.

So for me, everybody makes decisions all day long. All of us lose track at times, some more than others. And all of us report what's going on with less than complete recall and candor.

How, then, can we lift the veil of another person's decisional activity? Look at all the difficulties.

1. People vary in recognizing their decisions (especially their rejections and their habitual acceptances).
2. People draw the line differently between what they will and won't allow as things they could do anything about.
3. People vary in their willingness to admit to and discuss their decisions.
4. People vary in recognizing their own rationalizations (demalogical transformations) of reasons for their actions.
5. People vary in how much they rationalize their decisions as they communicate them.

Here lies one of the great advantages of comparative demalogics. You can often use it to see the decisional approach other people are taking even when they don't see it themselves. Whether used consciously or unconsciously, the demalogics work the same way.

So, if you can spot other people's demalogics (more on this [in the next installment]), you obtain an inside edge. You can then tell, for example, what kinds of facts and concerns will be relevant for those deciders and what kinds of errors tend most to trip them. You can also see what you are up against in case you attempt to persuade them to use another set of demalogics.

---

### WHO'S CRAZY?

Psychosis has frequently been defined as the loss of control over choices. Yet psychotherapists sometimes achieve results by assuming just the opposite, that people actually decide to go mad.

★ ★ ★ ★ ★

She had been in the hospital about four years at that point . . . and had a long history of treatment, so I asked her, "What are the advantages to being crazy?"

She replied, "There are lots of advantages." She then listed the advantages: 1) she never had to worry about a job; 2) she didn't have to worry about dates . . . ; 3) she could do and say anything she wanted . . . .

So I said, "Well, under these circumstances, what do you want to do?"

She said, "I'd like to leave the hospital."

I asked her, "What for? Look at all the tremendous payoffs you have."...

But at that first session she decided that she was going to get out of that hospital. She asked me, "How can I do it?"

I said, "It's easy. All you have to do is act sane. The only difference between you and us [the staff of the hospital] is that you act crazy and we act sane. If you want to get out, act sane.". . .

And that's what happened. . . .

Some time later, she met a man she liked and they were married, and she had a lovely baby. She told me that after the child was born she began to get sick again, but then she remembered . . . and said to herself, "You can either go crazy or you can be the kind of wife and mother that you really want to be." And she decided to become the wife and mother she really wanted to be.

I find that people who have been psychotic seem to recognize this idea of decision better than many people in the profession. [At a conference in San Francisco] I described some of my cases, and some of the professionals there said I was crazy. But a lot of the crazies who had been through psychosis said, "Of course!" They could get up and say when they had decided to be crazy, and under what circumstances they had made that decision. They got up and said when they decided to go straight. Now, this is not as simple as it seems, because one of the problems is that when people make the decision to be crazy, it really takes over and becomes extremely difficult to reverse.

Harold Greenwald, *Direct Decision Therapy*. San Diego: EdITS, 1973. Copyright, Dr. Harold Greenwald. Reprinted by permission.

### ANSWERS TO THE QUESTIONS ON DEMALOGICAL PATHS

The most defensible routes (with demalogics italicized for a bonus) appear to be:

1. (re water) 1-5-11-13-21-22-*24*.
2. (re red light) 1-5-11-13-*14*-15-17-19-21-25-*34*.
3. (re job offer) 1-5-11-13-*14*-15-17-19-*20*-21-25-26-27-30-32-33-*38*.
4. (re divorce) 1-*2*-3-(dissolving)-*4*-*5*-*6*-7-8-(*9* or *10*)-11-*12*(your vows)-13-*14*-15-*16*(your routine procedures and tastes)-17(dissolving)-*18*-19-21-25-(*34*, if you just can't accept divorce)-26-(*35*, if you just must be free)-27-30-32-33-*38*.
5. (re back-up manager) 1-*2*-3-*4*-5-*6*-7-8-*10*-11-13-*14*-15-*16*-17-*18*(a new staff position)-19-*20*-21-25-26-27-29(or 30)-32-33-*37*.
6. (re appeal) 1-*2*-3-5-*6*-7-8-*9*(assuming you are with the majority)-11-*12*-13-*14*-15-*16*-17-19-21-25-26-27-29-32-33-(*37* or *38*, which you would then, in keeping with #*16*, express primarily in responsive terms).

[To be continued. In the next installment: more views from the summit of comparative demalogics—responsibility, verbal clues and levers, the complete decider, conclusion.]

# *Commentary eight*

[EDITOR'S FOREWORD: MacNeal's formulation of twenty-odd decision-making logics (demalogics) creates the possibility of an entirely new synthesis of psychologies.

It is well known that one "feature of modern psychology—as distinct from the established sciences—is that its various schools, systems, and orientations seem to exist largely as independent principalities, distantly related, if not completely separated from one another conceptually and semantically."† Studying the theories relating to conditioned responses, behavioral reinforcement, psychoanalysis, language acquisition, and goal-directed behaviors, for example, may well leave one academically wiser but more confused than before. How could so many theories that don't fit together, that have such different terminologies, and that criticize each other so effectively, all be right?

The *Master Atlas* has permitted me to look at these disparate psychological theories more comfortably. The responsive pattern (if x happens, do y) supports the stimulus-response approach. The absolute pattern (if you like x, do x) fits with hedonistic reinforcements. The goal-directed pattern (to get x, do y) supports motivational psychology and self-actualization theories. These three and other demalogics, all apparently prewired into our brains, provide different meanings for perceptions, which fits with cognitive psychology.

I haven't worked it all out, of course, but our multiple demalogics provide both varied psychological phenomena to study and varied theories to explain them with. This double effect makes clearer why each psychological school

---

†David N. Robinson, *Systems of Modern Psychology* (New York: Columbia University Press, 1979), p. 17. See also Douglas J. Steinberg's review in *Et cetera*, Spring 1981.

explains only some phenomena well. It turns the confusion of multiple psychological theories into a natural development.

A similar lack of coherence appears to disjoint all social science. Perhaps multiple demalogics, arrayed on seven levels of structural complexity, might just help clarify social science in general.

Here is a highly condensed synopsis of the first seven installments (*Et cetera*, Fall 1987 through Spring 1989):

We use demamaps (*de*cision-*ma*king *maps*) with various structures (demalogics) on seven levels: (1) *subdecisional events*, (2) *basic demapatterns* [one action, one reason], (3) *compound demapatterns* [one action, multiple reasons], (4) *basic linkages* between decisions [doable by one decider], (5) *interpersonal linkages*, (6) self-reinforcing *systems* of interpersonal decisions, and (7) *comparative demalogics*.

Subdecisional events (level 1) include *situations* (what we can't change) and *alternaquences* (what we can do or affect, from *altern*ative and *conse-quences*). Verbally splitting "actions" from "consequences" induces a presumptuous elementalism; we cannot have one without the other. All basic demapatterns (level 2) except the originative exhibit this elementalism. So does the scorecard pattern at level 3.

| Demapattern | Formula |
|---|---|
| *absolute* | If you like action x, do x. |
| *action-comparative* | If you prefer action x to action y, do x. |
| *responsive* | If situation x occurs, do action y. |
| *goal-directed* | To get goal x, do action y. |
| *originative* | If you prefer alternaquence x to alternaquence y, do x. |
| *scorecard* | If x's good points outweigh its bad points, or if x's net score beats y's net score, do x. |

We mostly use the first two patterns for simpler personal matters, underestimate use of the responsive, overestimate the goal-directed, and let elementalistic "values" take us past the originative pattern to the scorecard. Each pattern has uses and dangers.

*Basic linkages* (level 4) include the *transformative* (pattern shifts), *recursive* (decisions about decisions), and *allocative* (effect of action on availability of other actions). *Interpersonal linkages* (level 5) include the *propositional* (actions proposed to other persons), *mutual* (alike actions deciders can't take solo), *reciprocal* (unlike actions deciders exchange), and *organizational* (actions that found, staff, or animate extrahuman demaunits).

Comparative demalogics (level 7) has thus far revealed decisions outnumbering demalogics, a way to pick demalogics, how error and forecasts depend on demalogics, and how much people's demaconsciousness varies.

We now continue at level 7 in the broad, personal, and semantic vein fostered by comparative demalogics ...]

# 8. More on applying demalogics

**Responsibility**

Givers and accepters of responsibility often find themselves in a demalogical tug of war.

Givers want to be able to judge performance on every demamap and with the broadest view of decision-making activity. If they ask to have the factory painted, they want the safety rules followed, the painting completed on time, a handsome result, one they can live with a long time, a model for the next assignment, at a reasonable cost, with no detracting side effects, and more. They want no limitations on the demalogical standards they can apply.

**Table 24    Demalogically loaded questions**

| Question | Map Presumed |
|---|---|
| But will they like it? | absolute |
| Do you think that's fair? | responsive |
| What are you trying to achieve? | goal-directed |
| Won't your preferences change? | originative |
| What are the drawbacks? | scorecard |
| How can we make that a rule? | transformative |
| Who said you could decide? | recursive |
| Why do you waste your time? | allocative |
| Shall we fight about it? | mutual |
| What could you get for it? | reciprocal |
| Shouldn't you appoint someone? | organizational |

Accepters of responsibility, however, would be happier with just one standard: following the rules, *or* completing on time, *or* matching a color, *or* doing the best they can within a given time, *or* cost. They recognize the dangers in allowing themselves to be held accountable in all the demalogics. Therefore, they want to limit the scope of judgment and the types of questions that could be brought to bear.

Actually, I don't select menus. I just turn spits.

Executives sometimes delegate the broadest responsibility in the briefest form. "It's your baby." Note the demalogical implications of "your" and "baby." What broader responsibility using more demamaps do most people ever have?

The extent to which we would limit the responsibilities we accept shows up best in statements after the event. "I was only following your instructions." "I was just trying to get the job done on time." "I only wanted to save money." Note the demalogical implications of "only" and "just." How better could we announce that we had put other demamaps aside?

The middle ground, where we give or accept more direction and more specific standards, is a vast subject of its own. To give more direction opens a demalogical Pandora's box. Each new instruction invokes a demamap that stresses some kinds of responsibility and ignores others. Corrective efforts may succeed only in making simple requests read like government contracts.

**Verbal Clues And Levers**

At least one word in ten carries a demalogical implication. Anyone who grasps these implications can use them both as clues to what other people are thinking and as levers to influence them.

Because we live in a sea of words that we take for granted, we often fail to recognize the subtle and pervasive power of language.

> **THE TYRANNY OF WORDS**
>
> Human beings ... are very much at the mercy of the particular language which has become the medium of expression for their society. It is quite an illusion to imagine that one adjusts to reality essentially without the use of language and that language is merely an incidental means of solving specific problems of communication or reflection. The fact of the matter is that the 'real world' is to a large extent unconsciously built up on the language habits of the group....
> Edward Sapir, "The Status of Linguistics as a Science," *Language*, Vol. 5, p. 209.
> We dissect nature along lines laid down by our native languages.... The categories and types that we isolate from the world of phenomena we do not find there because they stare every observer in the face; on the contrary, the world is presented in a kaleidoscopic flux of impressions which has to be organized by our minds—and this means largely by the linguistic systems in our minds.
> Benjamin Lee Whorf, "Science and Linguistics," *The Technology Review*, Vol. 42, No.6.
> *The power of terminology*, because of its structural implications, is well known in science, but is entirely disregarded in our daily neuro-linguistic habits.
> Alfred Korzybski, *Science and Sanity*, xxxvi.

Consider the simple statement, "Tomorrow is your mother's birthday." If we treat this as just a factual declaration, we miss the point. The demalogical significance of these words far outweighs their factual aspect. Interpreting the statement in the responsive pattern yields:
1. There is a situation (namely, tomorrow is your mother's birthday).
2. Certain courses of action (namely, observances) fit that situation and are expected.
3. What are *you* going to do?

The original statement, apparently simple and factual, actually operates as a behavioral lever in the responsive pattern. Add to this the fact that embarrassment and guilt may follow an inadequate or fake response, and we can see why people sometimes regard such innocent-looking statements as psychological blackmail.

Of course, unless we interpret the statement responsively, the leverage disappears. (How different the words sound if you are just trying to figure out to whom an unaddressed, gift-wrapped package might belong.) How, then, does the statement tell us—given no special context—to take it responsively? The answer is that three of the words ("birthday," "mother's," and "your") label situations for which we have separately—and long ago—learned appropriate responses. The other two words ("tomorrow" and "is") assert when the situation in this case will arise.

This general responsive form occurs repeatedly. "Dinner is at seven o'clock." "That's dad's chair." "I'm tired." "Window closed." Interpreted responsively, these statements say, "Be on time," "Please don't sit there," "Let me rest," and "Try the next teller."

Now take the common utterance, "What's your problem?" This question summons the goal-directed pattern because that is the demalogic in which "problems" generally appear. Therefore we interpret the question as saying:

1. There is a desired state (goal).
2. Something is blocking the way.
3. What is it?
4. Overcome it.

If the desired state is peace and quiet, then the question means "Why are you making so much noise? Stop it." If the desired state is completed work, then the question means "What's holding up the job? Lick it." This formula is so standard that the word "problem" in almost any context calls for a goal-directed demamap. "The pollution problem." "The unemployment problem." "The nuclear problem." "Thank you all for getting here so quickly. Here's the problem."

Spotting verbal clues to demalogics helps us understand how others are looking at decisions, both their own and the ones they want us to make. We can then knowingly deal with both the surface statements and the implied demalogic, which may or may not be the best one for the circumstances. "There is no problem. The program works. We were drawing straws for the honor and pleasure of advising you that it finally runs without a hitch. Congratulations." In demalogical translation this says, "The goal-directed approach no longer applies. The situation is that the goal has been reached. This situation calls for responsive ceremony and absolute pleasure, thanks to you."

Understanding how verbal levers work—that they call up particular demalogics—gives us more control over our own decisions and more influence over those of others. Such leverage can make a substantial difference, because different demalogics have different uses, as Table 25 [ahead overleaf] reminds us.

Tuning one's ear to hear demalogical clues in context takes practice. Here are a few terms to try out as a warm-up. Just put each term into an appropriate sentence.

>absolute: like, detest, fun, disgusting (for example, "I like ice cream.")
>responsive: my, Sunday, blame, boss
>goal-directed: aim, need, plan, hurdle, fail
>originative: prefer, rather, all in all
>scorecard: pluses, drawback, outweigh
>transformative: codify, goal-setting, excuse
>allocative: budget, resources, mismanage

# Verbal clues and levers

"Holmes, how ever did you deduce that your new client had recently read <u>Mac Neal's Master Atlas of Decision Making?</u>"

"Elementary, my dear Watson. He said he was so **absolutely delighted** with my **proposal** to establish a **reciprocal allocation of resources** that he straightway **directed** himself toward the **goal** of **transforming** his **preference** for **originating** that **course of action** into an **appropriate response**. Only then did he compose himself enough to say yes."

Now, here's a quiz for the master detective. (The demalogics represented are not limited to those in this chapter.)

---

### CAN YOU INTERPRET THESE CLUES?
Name the likely demalogics behind these words.
1. aimless
2. although
3. bargain
4. cheat
5. duel
6. franchise
7. orders
8. pretext
9. reconsider
10. squander

(Answers on last page of this installment)

**Table 25**      **Some uses of selected demalogics**

| Demalogic | Typical Uses |
|---|---|
| Absolute | enjoying oneself; developing a style; avoiding distastes |
| Responsive | promoting standardization, simplification, habit formation, detailed compliance, and precise coordination; dismissing consequences; minimizing doubts; reducing demaconsciousness; controlling others |
| Goal-directed | promoting general cooperation, maximum effort, and enthusiasm; finding new answers; dismissing situations, rules, and side effects; tolerating actions; directing specialists |
| Originative | previewing alternaquences; selecting courses in unprecedented circumstances; transcending contradictory rules, goals, and tastes; promoting demaconsciousness |
| Scorecard | combining separately inconclusive criteria; exploring different points of view |
| Transformative | creating rules, goals, tastes, excuses, and limited theories of behavior |
| Allocative | determining which actions most enhance the availability of other actions |

**Not Just Words**

Not everyone who talks a good game plays well.

Some good talkers develop into facile overpromisers and Monday morning quarterbacks. Other well-practiced talkers have thought long and hard about many things, and perhaps they could stop ocean pollution or could have averted a recent war. Then why do we sometimes hesitate to trust them with such important but ordinary tasks as mailing the rent check?

Becoming a skillful demaplayer takes practice, of course. The question is "practicing what?" The answer is practicing an action orientation, the persistent personal bent to see that decisions are made, that something is done, some action is accepted or rejected. Not just talked about, but done.

Skillful demaplayers readily find useful courses of action hidden from others. They seem to know when to accept and reject actions, when to postpone decision, when to seize the moment, when to listen, how to cooperate, and how to bargain with good talk. In short, they make it look easy.

Unfortunately, some of the ways we talk about things virtually rule out an action orientation. We lead ourselves astray.

Take proposals, for instance. To be operative, a proposal must contain a course of action available to the person to whom it is proposed. Thus, my saying, "please reread the definition just given," is operative. I have communicated it to you and you can do it. But if I were to say here, "you should never have started reading this book," that would be inoperative. I am too late. And if I were to ask you to call me at the office in a hundred years, that would also be inoperative. Unless medicine makes unprecedented advances, you will be too late.

Similarly, consider value judgments. To promote an action orientation, they must relate to available actions. Many don't. You and I may agree that the world would be better off if Adolf Hitler, for example, had never been born, but it refers to no action available to either of us.

Such disengaged value judgments have their place. I use them to express sympathy and regret, to confirm my human feelings. Wouldn't it be better, for example, if we had all been taught early in life how to soothe each other with inoperative proposals? I wish I had been. (You see what I mean?)

The action-orientation trick here is to stay alive to the difference between spilt milk and tomorrow's choices, between operative and inoperative proposals, between engaged and disengaged value judgments.

Isn't this weather dreadful? First it's too hot; then it's too cold. And I hate the rain every weekend. What's the use of planning anything? Who knows what will ever happen? Look at the mess in city hall. You'd think there'd be a way to keep politicians honest. Somebody really should do something about that. I mean it. Well, at least they gave us a good park system. I guess we have to be thankful for whatever we can get. The trouble is some people get more than their share. And they still want more. It's wrong and I'll never understand it.

Any persons you happen to know who talk like this are on vacation from action orientation. If they don't sense that their string of disengaged value judgments is just a way of blowing off steam, if they confuse it with decision making, they're on a really long vacation. They're away spinning their demawheels.

Even sensible and well-intentioned people can blow their action-orientation opportunities. We sometimes get so caught up in the reasons for action—by focusing on situations, rules, goals, consequences, likes, dislikes, preferences, and their interplay—that we neglect to act. We can always find many more reasons than actions to think about; just whirl through the demalogics. Resolving all such reasons into one grand harmonious scheme is probably impossible, even if we had the time. Yet that resolution is what some people seek, and while they seek their decisions languish.

Reasons matter, yes, but reasoning alone, without action, is like training for a race without running. Would you lend your car to someone who knew all about it but who had never actually driven?

## The Complete Decider

A complete decider would know all the demalogics and knowingly pick the best ones for the circumstances.

That said, we can see that few complete deciders dwell among us. Most deciders make do with limited ability in a few demalogics, which they apply unknowingly. Even our "experts" (for example, accountants, doctors, engineers, and lawyers) typically master only a few demalogics, which they then apply to limited subject matter.

People who have achieved success at their specialty find that their habitual demalogics don't work elsewhere. Even good accountants, doctors, engineers, and lawyers can steer themselves into domestic, financial, legal, and organizational messes. So do successful artists, business executives, and teachers.

Skill in a particular demalogic, no matter how great, does not translate into general demacompetence. Each demalogic must be mastered separately. The decider must learn through comparative demalogics when best to apply each. Only then do we have an all-around, complete, decider.

Fortunately, many people have progressed a good way down the road to general competence. Most deciders already know something about many demalogics simply by using the vocabularies associated with each. They already "know" that "guilt" involves breaking responsive rules, "victory" depends on goal-directed efforts, "budgets" allocate resources, and "excuses" can transform reasons. Most deciders have a practical grasp of the particular demalogics used in their occupations. Everybody knows something about organizations.

Most people, however, don't know how far they have gone down the road toward comparative demalogics and general competence. They don't even know there is such a road.

These pages, of course, can help chart and illuminate the road to comparative demalogics. Travelers can gauge their progress and redirect their efforts in the light of this new map.

The more demalogics we master, and the more we understand comparative demalogics, the more competent as decision makers will we become.

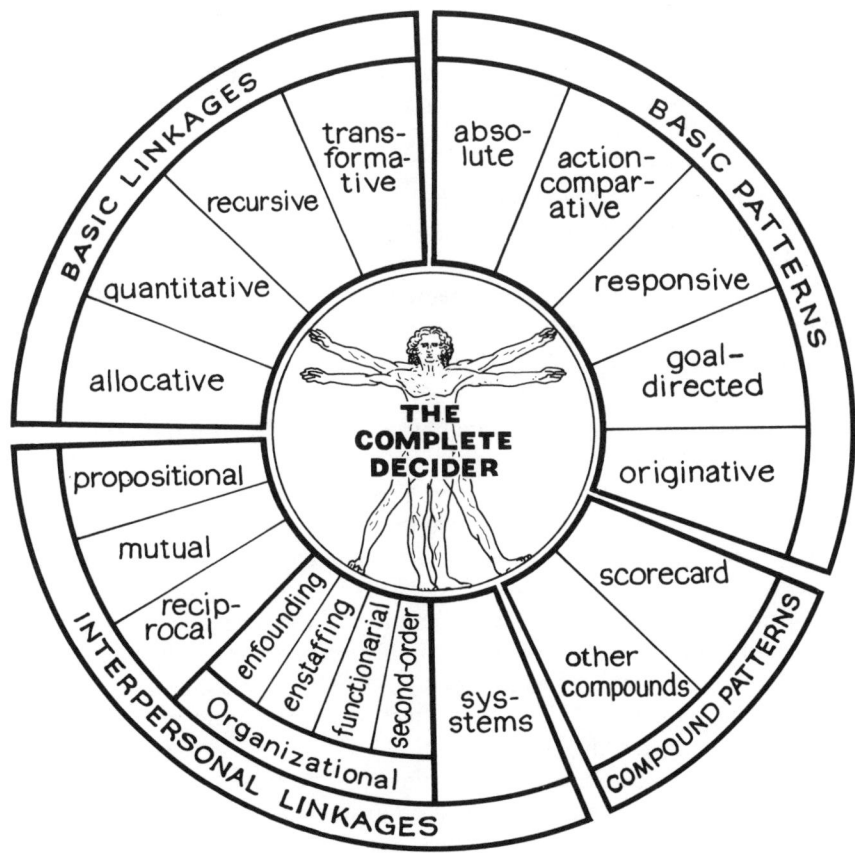

## "Not All"

Because a map does not represent all the territory, general semanticists like to close with a reminder that they have not said everything. Even their noted journal, first published in 1943 and still going strong, carries the title *Et cetera*.

General semanticists use the reminder positively, not as an excuse or false modesty. They know they haven't said everything. They want to make sure the readers know.

Among the matters *not* included in these pages are:
1. The quantitative linkage
2. Full discussion of any demalogic
3. Advice on any specific decision
4. Controversial issues and "values"
5. The biological underpinnings of demalogics
6. Cross-cultural analysis of demalogics
7. Which academic disciplines promote which demalogics
8. A curriculum based on comparative demalogics
9. The demalogics of power and control
10. Et cetera

If you have been alert, you may have noted a bigger omission, namely the failure to forecast the alternaquence that originates with the study of comparative demalogics. Lest I be embarrassed by reference to the first sentence of the page on "Forecasting" [in the previous installment], let's remedy this omission right now.

The slowly growing circles (in number, but fast growing in annual percentage increase) of users of comparative demalogics report personal success in organizing their own demahabits, some decisions they are happy with, and an advantage in dealing with other people.

> My aim is not to be a prophet, but to analyse different structural and linguistic semantic issues underlying all human activities, and so to produce material which may help mankind to *select* their lot *consciously*.
> Alfred Korzybski, *Science and Sanity*, p. 273.

I wonder what a world would be like in which, say, one person in a hundred understood and could use comparative demalogics. Would the users feel they had an unfair advantage? Would the users do better personally? socially? economically? Would they make more, and regret fewer, decisions? Would the users recognize and communicate more rapidly with each other than with other people? Would they come to regard absolute, responsive, and goal-directed decisions as valuable but blind-sided shortcuts? Would the usage of comparative demalogics then take off?

If usage spread to one person in ten, would strife be reduced? Litigation costs reduced? Would we experiment with new governmental demastructures? Would accidents decline? Drug abuse? Crime?

How about universal usage in a later generation? Would we have more command of the feelings (duty, honor, prejudice, purpose, love, and hate) that depend on specific demamaps? And yet still care deeply?

Yes. I think so.

As alternaquences go, you know how I've decided. I'm with Isabella. We must explore. Especially decision making. What if a competitor got there first?

We have now truly reached the end of this guided journey to the new demaworld. Many strange sights and sounds and symbols have we seen. Thanks for coming along.

[Nevertheless, to be continued. In the next installment: a structural summary and a glossary.

---

### DISCLAMATION

Publication of this work by the International Society for General Semantics and quotation from Alfred Korzybski's *Science and Sanity* does not mean that the author endorses everything Korzybski said.

Serious general semanticists typically regard Korzybski as an important pioneer in showing how profoundly sanity relates to semantic habits fostered by language, even though much of what he wrote now has only historical interest.* If they who stand in part on Korzybski's shoulders cannot see much farther than he, then he was no giant.

Time will also make this note superfluous. Does anyone fear that the Hippocratic oath binds doctors to practice ancient Greek medicine?

---

*See, for examples, Anatol Rapoport, "What I Think Korzybski Thought—And What I Think About It," *Et cetera* December 1976, and Neil Postman, *Conscientious Objections* (New York: Knopf, 1988).

---

### ANSWERS TO THE WORD CLUES

1. goal-directed (a disparaging judgment that behavior is not goal-directed)
2. scorecard (you are about to hear the reasons that are outweighed by other reasons)
3. reciprocal (an agreed exchange, a judgment that an exchange is favorable)
4. responsive (a disparaging judgment that behavior did not follow the rules)
5. mutual (a joining in like action that neither decider could carry out alone)
6. organizational second-order (one way a business spawns other businesses)
7. propositional (as evidenced by the possibility of disobedience)
8. transformative (reasons for action other than the real reasons)
9. recursive (decision to reopen a decision)
10. allocative (a judgment that an action foolishly reduces the availability of other actions dependent on the same resource)

# Appendices

*Commentary nine*
**A. Summary of demalogical structures**

**B. Glossary**

*Commentary ten*
**C. At the demalogical helm** *(a textual explication)*

**D. Sample demalogical dictionary entries**

**E. Demalogical thesaurus**

**F. Sources**


**Index**

# Commentary nine

[EDITOR'S FOREWORD: The eight previous installments of this series, spanning two years of *Et cetera*, have covered considerable ground. The two appendices making up this installment provide two usefully different summaries.

The first appendix summarizes the demalogical structures. It covers all seven levels and pulls together the definitions, formulas, and diagrams from all earlier installments. The second appendix summarizes in a glossary the specialized terms used in the *Master Atlas*. The structural summary permits review by demalogical level; the glossary, by alphabetical lookup.

I have already noted in the previous installment that psychology and other social sciences each appear to entertain only one or a few demalogics (many psychologists favor the goal-directed pattern, economists stress the allocative linkage, etc.). The *Master Atlas*, of course, takes a broader approach and notes ways we can use and misuse each demalogic.

I would now like to make a modest suggestion. Whatever your field, why not challenge its conventional wisdom with regard to its demalogical limitations? Mathematicians challenged Euclid's parallel postulate and found totally new, but logically consistent and useful, geometries. As a psychologist, for example, might you not gain by dropping the axiom that all behavior (or all rational cognitive behavior) fits a single explanatory framework? Try regarding each demalogic as useful somewhere. Does not this seeming complication really agree with experience and might it not lead ultimately to greater simplicity? Think what could happen if each field were to drop its parochial assumptions regarding demalogics and reexamine itself in terms of their whole range.

Now, consider another possibility. It's been said that each field and each school within each field specializes in the phenomena found to fit the explanations it happens to favor. Then investigators in each field would tend to ignore the phenomena that don't fit their demalogics, wouldn't they? It's conceivable that those who expand their lists of allowable demalogics will discover important phenomena and principles that their associates have overlooked.]

# A. Summary of demalogical structures

This appendix gathers in one place the demalogical structures developed in different places in the text. A few details (especially for the compound patterns and the quantitative linkage) and a few notes have been added to round out this presentation.

A decision is the acceptance or rejection of a course of action to be taken and a proposal is the putting forth of an action for acceptance or rejection. Proposals have structures analogous to decisions. To avoid repetition, proposers and proposals are not further mentioned in this summary except as needed for clarity.

"Demalogic" (*decision-ma*king *logic*) is the short way to refer to the particular kind of reasoning that goes with each different kind of demamap used by deciders. Such demamaps in total portray seven different levels of demalogical structure.

| Level | Demalogics |
|---|---|
| Level 1. Subdecisional events: events that are not in themselves decisions | situation   alternaquence<br>course of action<br>consequence |
| Level 2. Basic patterns: one action in relation to one reason | absolute   responsive   originative<br>action-comparative   goal-directed |
| Level 3. Compound patterns: one action in relation to two or more reasons | uniform   multiform   scorecard   sequential |
| Level 4. Basic linkages: interacting decisions of one decider | transformative recursive quantitative allocative |
| Level 5. Interpersonal linkages: interacting decisions of two or more deciders | propositional mutual reciprocal organizational<br>enfounding<br>enstaffing<br>functionarial<br>second-order |
| Level 6. Systems: self-reinforcing continuities of interpersonal decisions | recursive-functionarial-responsive |
| Level 7. Comparative demalogics: comparative study of demalogics | comparisons of demalogics at all levels |

105

The seven levels are intended to be mutually exclusive and exhaustive of the possible demalogical structural levels. Similarly, the demalogics at each level are intended to be mutually exclusive and exhaustive of the possible demalogical structures at that level.

Level 1. Subdecisional events: events that are not in themselves decisions, including
    1.1  Situation: events a decider cannot affect in a particular case
    1.2  Alternaquence: events a decider can affect in a particular case, including
    1.21  Course of action (action): what a decider is surely able to do in a particular case (as a practical certainty, barring philosophical doubt, etc.).
    1.22  Consequence: what a decider is not surely able to do (or bring about) in a particular case

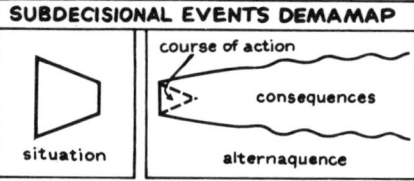

Note: Situations and alternaquences are mutually exclusive and exhaust the class of events. Courses of action and consequences have a fuzzier boundary, but they are also mutually exclusive and exhaust the class of alternaquences.

Level 2. Basic demapatterns: various internal demastructures, each consisting of one action in relation to one reason within one decision, including
    2.1  Absolute pattern: acceptance (or rejection) of an action for itself alone [i.e., apart from situations and consequences]

| Pattern | Formula | ABSOLUTE DEMAMAP |
|---|---|---|
| Absolute | If you like x, do x. | course of action ▷ |

    2.2  Action-comparative pattern: acceptance (or rejection) of an action as preferred (or not) in itself to another action in itself [i.e., apart from likes, dislikes, situations, and consequences]

| Pattern | Formula | ACTION-COMPARATIVE DEMAMAP |
|---|---|---|
| Action-comparative | If you prefer x to y, do x. | courses of action ▷ ▷ |

# Summary of demalogical structures

2.3 Responsive pattern: acceptance (or rejection) of an action as fitting (or not) a situation

| Pattern | Formula |
|---|---|
| Responsive | If x occurs, do y. |

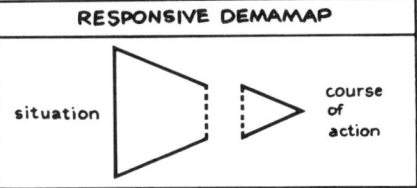

2.4 Goal-directed pattern: acceptance (or rejection) of an action for the sake of a desired consequence (goal)

| Pattern | Formula |
|---|---|
| Goal-directed | To get x, do y. |

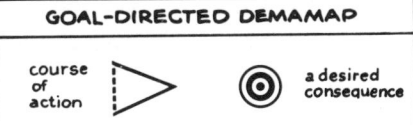

2.5 Originative pattern: acceptance (or rejection) of an alternaquence as preferred (or not) in itself to another alternaquence in itself and in total [i.e., apart from judgment on any individual elements thereof]

| Pattern | Formula |
|---|---|
| Originative | If you prefer alternaquence x to alternaquence y, do x. |

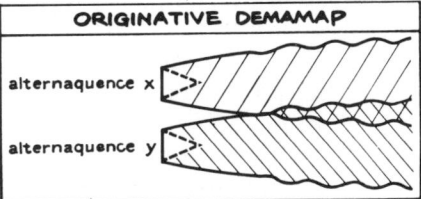

Note: The five basic patterns are mutually exclusive, disparate (they cannot be reduced to each other), and exhaustive of the ways in which subdecisional events can be related one at a time to an action chosen (or rejected) within a decision.

Level 3. Compound demapatterns: various internal demastructures, each consisting of one action in relation to two or more reasons within one decision, including

    3.1 Uniform pattern: acceptance (or rejection) of an action for concurring reasons in the same pattern

    3.2 Multiform pattern: acceptance (or rejection) of an action for concurring reasons in different patterns

Note: The diagram at right illustrates only one of many possibilities

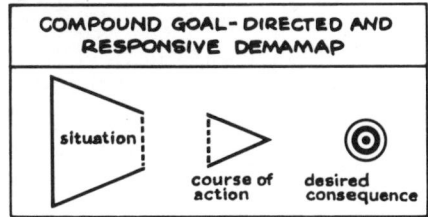

3.3 Scorecard pattern: acceptance (or rejection) of an action because (1) it has more points in its favor than against it or (2) its net balance of points beats that of alternatives

| Pattern | Formula |
|---|---|
| Scorecard 1* | If x's good points outweigh its bad points, do x. |
| Scorecard 2 | If x's net score beats y's net score, do x. |

*diagrammed at right

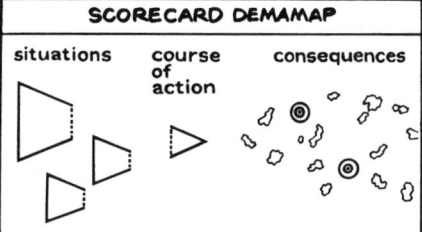

3.4 Sequential pattern: acceptance (or rejection) of a course of action through a stepwise procedure in which a different demapattern may be used at each step

Note: The four compound patterns (with their many variants) are mutually exclusive and exhaust the ways in which multiple reasons can be related to an action chosen (or rejected) within a decision.

Note: Levels 2 and 3 together, by exhausting the ways in which a decider can relate action to one or more reasons within one decision, also exhaust the possible internal structural arrangements one decider can make within one decision.

Level 4. Basic demalinkages: various ways in which a single decider can recast decisions into different forms and link decisions to each other, including

4.1 Transformative linkage: the various ways that decisions can be transformed from one demapattern into another

| Demalogic | Identifying Linkage |
|---|---|
| Transformative | conversion of a decision from one to another demapattern |

4.2 Quantitative linkage: the various ways that decisions can be cast into numerical terms

| Demalogic | Identifying linkage |
|---|---|
| Quantitative | casting any part of a decision in quantitative terms |

Note: Quantification does not create new demapatterns, but does create such possibilities as (1) finer distinctions in defining situations, actions, likes, dislikes, preferences, consequences, goals, and alternaquences, (2) finer weighting of reasons in compound patterns, (3) finer coordination of steps in sequential patterns, (4) the derivation of courses of action from numerical facts and criteria, and (5) finer interactions between decisions (in the demalinkages listed below).

# Summary of demalogical structures

    4.3  Recursive linkage: the various ways that a decision can be made about another decision

| Demalogic | Identifying Linkage |
|---|---|
| Recursive | decision about a decision |

    4.4  Allocative linkage: the various ways that a course of action in a decision can affect the availability of other actions

| Demalogic | Identifying Linkage |
|---|---|
| Allocative | effect of one action on availability of another action |

Note: The four basic linkages are mutually exclusive and intended to exhaust the ways in which a single decider can recast or link decisions. A propositional linkage (see 5.1 below) could be included as a fifth basic linkage, if we wished to regard a lone decider's deliberations as self-directed proposals.

Level 5. Interpersonal linkages: ways in which deciders (or proposers and deciders) can engage each other in making decisions, including

    5.1  Propositional linkage: the various ways that one person can propose an action to another person [or demaunit, see 5.4 below]

| Demalogic | Identifying Linkage |
|---|---|
| Propositional | course of action proposed by one person to another |

    5.2  Mutual linkage: the various ways that two or more deciders can take like actions that they could not carry out alone

| Demalogic | Identifying Linkage |
|---|---|
| Mutual | like actions by deciders that none could take alone |

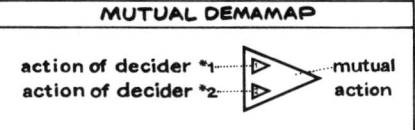

    5.3  Reciprocal linkage: the various ways that a decider can take action in exchange for a different action by another decider

| Demalogic | Identifying Linkage |
|---|---|
| Reciprocal | Unlike actions that deciders take in exchange |

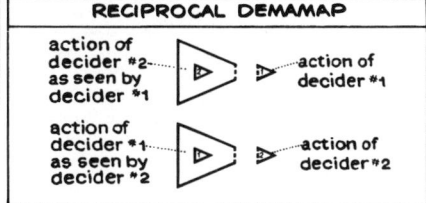

    5.4  Organizational linkages: the various ways that decisions are made involving extrahuman demaunits (organizations, demagroups, demapositions), including

5.41 Enfounding linkage: the various ways that extrahuman demaunits can be begun or ended

| Demalogic | Identifying Linkage |
|---|---|
| Enfounding | action founding or terminating an extrahuman demaunit |

5.42 Enstaffing linkage: the various ways that extrahuman demaunits can be staffed

| Demalogic | Identifying Linkage |
|---|---|
| Enstaffing | action staffing or destaffing an extrahuman demaunit |

5.43 Functionarial linkage: the various ways that an extrahuman demaunit's staff can function in animating that demaunit

| Demalogic | Identifying Linkage |
|---|---|
| Functionarial | action by the staff animating an extrahuman demaunit |

5.44 Second-order linkage: the various ways that an extrahuman demaunit can use the enfounding and enstaffing linkages with regard to further demaunits

| Demalogic | Identifying Linkage |
|---|---|
| Second-order | functionarial enfounding or enstaffing a further demaunit |

Note: The interpersonal linkages (5.1-5.44) are intended to be mutually exclusive (although the boundary between 5.2 and 5.3 can be particularly fuzzy) and to exhaust the ways in which deciders (or proposers and deciders) can engage each other in decisions, taken one linkage at a time.

Level 6. Demasystems: the various kinds of self-reinforcing networks of decisions and proposals based ultimately on responsive functionarial decisions about responsive functionarial decisions. Recursive functionarial responsiveness, or RFR, thus becomes the demasystem generating principle.

| Demalogic | Identifying Demalinkage |
|---|---|
| Demasystem | responsive functionarial decision about responsive functionarial decision |

Note: Further distinctions can be made between tightly constructed demasystems (like law) and looser demasystems (like etiquette), but all require some degree of RFR.

Note: Levels 4-6 exhaust the ways in which decisions or demapatterns can be linked to each other or transformed.

# Summary of demalogical structures

Level 7. Comparative demalogics: the various ways of comparing demalogics at the same or different levels, whether in decisions, decisional postmortems, dematraining, dematheory, stories, or whatever.

| Demalogic | Identifying Linkage |
|---|---|
| Comparative demalogics | comparison of one demalogic with another |

# B. Glossary

The definitions offered here cover only the contexts addressed in this book. Words set in *italics* are themselves defined in the Glossary.

**Absolute pattern:** *demapattern* in which a single *course of action* is selected or rejected because it is liked or disliked for itself

**Action:** see *course of action*

**Action-comparative pattern:** *demapattern* in which a *course of action* is selected as preferable in itself to another action in itself, or rejected as not preferable

**Action orientation:** degree of personal inclination to see that *decisions* are made, that something is done

**Act of deciding:** acceptance or rejection of a *course of action* (as distinct from any *reason* given)

**Allocative linkage:** effect of a *course of action* on the availability of another action

**Alternaquence:** *course of action* together with its *consequences* considered as an unsplittable unit; all the events a decider can affect in a given case

**Available course of action:** *course of action* that the decider can carry out with *practical certainty*

**Basic demalinkage:** any of the demalinkages (*transformative, quantitative, recursive,* or *allocative*) with which a single decider can recast *decisions* into different forms and link decisions to each other

**Basic demapattern:** any of the demapatterns (*absolute, action-comparative, responsive, goal-directed,* or *originative*) in which one *subdecisional event* can be related as one *reason* to one *course of action* in one *decision*

**Comparative demalogics:** 1. comparison of *demalogics*  2. theory that deciders have a choice of demalogics, each of which influences perceptions, attitudes, and behavior in its own way

**Complete decider:** decider who knows all the *demalogics* and knowingly picks the best ones for the circumstances

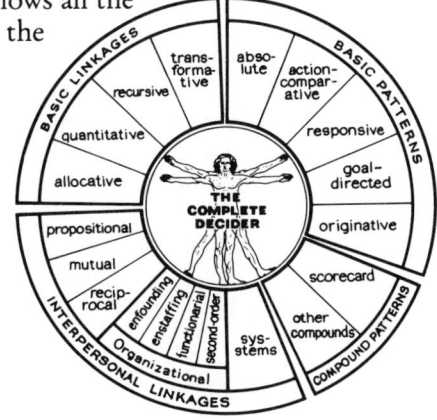

**Compound demapattern:** any of the demapatterns (*uniform, multiform, scorecard,* or *sequential*) in which two or more *reasons* can be related to one *course of action* in one *decision*

**Consequence:** event following without *practical certainty* from a *course of action*. In physical science a consequence (effect) can be a sure thing and in ordinary two-valued logic a consequence (implication) must be a sure thing. But in *demalogics* a consequence cannot be sure; for then it would become an *available course of action*.

**Course of action:** the part of an *alternaquence* that a decider presumably can do (bring about) with *practical certainty*. Compare *consequence*.

**Decision:** acceptance or rejection of a *course of action* to be taken

**Decision making:** noun, 1. making of a *decision* 2. study of how decisions are made. Compare next entry.

**Decision-making:** adjective, of or pertaining to *decision making*

**Dema-:** prefix, *decision-making*

**Demaformula:** recipe for a given *demapattern*

**Demalevel:** any of seven successive levels of *demastructure,* namely, (1) *subdecisional events,* (2) *basic demapatterns,* (3) *compound demapatterns,* (4) *basic demalinkages,* (5) *interpersonal demalinkages,* (6) *demasystems,* and (7) *comparative demalogics;* which in combination exhaust the demastructural possibilities

**Demalinkage:** any of the ways (*basic, interpersonal, demasystem,* or *comparative demalogics linkage*) of recasting or relating decisions to each other

**Demalogic:** a *demapattern, demalinkage, subdecisional event, demasystem,* or an instance of *comparative demalogics,* and the characteristic reasoning used therewith

**Demalogical specialization:** concentration on selected *demalogics,* as in different professions or within different company departments

**Demalogics:** 1. plural of *demalogic*   2. *comparative demalogics*

**Demamap:** symbolic representation of a given *demastructure*

**Demapattern:** 1. relationship of a *course of action* to the *reason(s)* for its acceptance or rejection within a *decision* or *proposal*   2. a *basic* or *compound demapattern*

**Demastructure:** any relationship of *demalevels, demalogics,* or demalogical parts

**Demasystem:** self-reinforcing network of regularly interacting *proposals* and *decisions*

**Demasystem linkage:** *responsive functionarial decision* about a responsive functionarial decision; *recursive functionarial responsiveness* (RFR)

**Demaunit:** general term for decider, whether human or *extrahuman*

**Direct preference:** preference for one *course of action* or *alternaquence* over others without reference to *situations, goals,* likes, or dislikes

**Disengaged value:** a *reason* exercised apart from any specific *decision* or *operative proposal,* often, but less clearly, referred to simply as *value*

**Elementalistic:** split symbolically (as in *"course of action"* from *"consequences"*) although not otherwise splittable. Compare *non-elementalistic.*

**Elementalistic value judgment:** *value judgment* on anything less than an *alternaquence*

**Enfounding linkage:** action founding or terminating an *extrahuman demaunit*

**Enstaffing linkage:** action staffing or destaffing an *extrahuman demaunit*

**Error:** see *usage error* and *oversight error*

**Extrahuman demaunit:** organization (association, partnership, corporation, legislature, club, etc.) or position therein able to make a *decision* for the organization or one of its parts

**Extrahuman linkage:** any of the linkages (*enfounding, enstaffing, functionarial,* or *second-order*) which involve *extrahuman demaunits.* Also known as *organizational demalinkage*

**Forecast:** anticipation of *consequences,* the lack of which is the commonest *oversight error*

**Functionarial linkage:** *decision* or *proposal* by a staff member on behalf of an organization

And now, speaking as your new Grand Pomegranate Elect, I have a few announcements.

# Glossary

**Goal:** the desired *consequence* of a *course of action*

**Goal-directed pattern:** *demapattern* in which a *course of action* is selected for the sake of a desired *consequence*

**Inoperative proposal:** *proposal* failing to meet one or more of the conditions for an *operative proposal*

**Interconnected decisions:** *decisions* joined by a *basic, interpersonal,* or *demasystem linkage*

**Interpersonal demalinkage:** any of the linkages (*propositional, mutual, reciprocal,* or *organizational*) requiring more than one decider

**Level of decision making:** see *demalevel*

**Linkage:** see *demalinkage*

**Loaded terms and phrases:** words or phrases owing their meaning to, and useful in identifying, particular *demalogics*

**Multiform pattern:** *compound demapattern* in which multiple *reasons* in different *basic demapatterns* all concur in the decision

**Mutual linkage:** *demalinkage* requiring a like *decision* by another decider. Includes conflict, competition, and cooperation.

**Non-elementalistic:** keeping together symbolically (as in "*alternaquence*") what cannot otherwise be split

**Non-elementalistic value judgment:** *direct preference* for an *alternaquence*

**Operative proposal:** *proposal* containing an *available course of action* for the decider to whom it is communicated

**Organizational demalinkage:** see *extrahuman demalinkage*

**Originative pattern:** *demapattern* in which a *previewed alternaquence* is accepted or rejected as preferred (or not) in itself in total to one or more other previewed alternaquences

**Oversight error:** error (like no *forecast* in the *responsive pattern*) caused by, but only visible from without, the *demalogic* being used

**Pattern:** see *demapattern*

**Practical certainty:** certainty, barring philosophical doubts, unforeseeable force majeure, and acts of God

**Preference:** see *direct preference*

**Preview:** imaginary experience through anticipation of an *alternaquence* apart from any *value judgment* thereon

**Primary rules:** *responsive rules* governing behavior, as distinguished in *demasystems* from *secondary rules* about rules

**Proposal:** invitation (whether in form a request, command, petition, directive, suggestion, offer, demand, claim, invitation, *rule,* bid, appeal, warning, or other) to make a *decision;* also the *course of action* proposed

**Propositional linkage:** *course of action* proposed by one *demaunit* to another

**Quantitative linkage:** any part of a *decision* or *proposal* cast into numbers

**Reason:** *subdecisional event* that is, or could be, given by a decider (as a *situation, consequence, goal,* like, dislike, *preference,* or compound thereof) for selecting or rejecting a *course of action*

**Reciprocal linkage:** *course of action* tied to another decider's course of action in exchange

**Recursive functionarial responsiveness** (RFR): *responsive functionarial decisions* about responsive functionarial decisions; the *demasystem* generating principle

**Recursive linkage:** *decision* about a decision, *proposal* about a proposal

**Responsive pattern:** *demapattern* in which a *course of action* is accepted as an appropriate response to a *situation*

**Responsive rule:** *proposal* in the form of a rule that a particular *course of action* is the appropriate response to a particular *situation*

**Rule:** see *responsive rule, primary rules, secondary rules*

**Scorecard pattern:** *demapattern* in which a *course of action* is accepted because it has (1) more points in its favor than against it or (2) a higher net balance of favorable points than an alternative action

**Secondary rules:** *responsive rules* about rules, as distinguished in *demasystems* from *primary rules* about behavior

# Glossary

**Second-order organizational linkage:** *functionarial* decision using the *enfounding* or *enstaffing linkage*

**Self-reflexive:** reflecting itself, recursive; the quality of symbol systems permitting talk about talk, the *recursive linkage,* etc.

**Sequential pattern:** *compound demapattern* in which one pattern at a time is used in successive steps to define, refine, or test a *course of action*

**Side effects:** *consequences* not relevant to a desired *goal*

**Situation:** event preceding or occurring independently of a given *decision*; all the events a decider cannot affect in a particular case

**Structural level:** see *demalevel*

**Subdecisional event:** any event (*situation, course of action, consequence,* or *alternaquence*) that is not in itself a *decision*

**System:** see *demasystem*

**Transformative linkage:** conversion of a *decision* or *proposal* from one to another *demapattern*

**Uniform pattern:** *compound demapattern* in which multiple *reasons* in the same *basic demapattern* all concur in the decision

**Usage error:** errors in using, and thus visible from within, a given *demalogic*

**Value:** slippery term when a presumed cause of decision and thus generally to be avoided. See *value judgment* and the glossary items listed there; also *elementalistic* and *non-elementalistic value judgment, error, loaded terms and phrases, rule*

**Value judgment:** 1. *act of deciding* (proposing)  2. *reason(s)* given  3. *disengaged value*

**Verbal split:** see *elementalistic*


[To be continued. In the next installment: a sample demalogical explication, a short demalogical thesaurus of ordinary English, an even shorter companion dictionary, and sources.]

## Commentary ten

[EDITOR'S FOREWORD: Last December I had a spirited discussion with MacNeal on a matter I now wish to share with you. It began when I made reference to the "complexity and difficulty" of his theory. He took exception, stating that his theory was really simple and easy, even though learning it was difficult for some people, and that one must distinguish the simplicity of a theory from the difficulty of learning it. I questioned whether such a separation could be made and reminded him that what might by now be easy for him certainly wasn't for me.

MacNeal then surprised me by stating that even after forty years, each new development of his theory costs him much effort. Only after laboriously trying things out one way and another and another would he finally discover a new and direct approach that clarified what had been so murky. "I was mistrained just like you," he said. "Nobody told me about decisional structure. I got a grab-bag of miscellaneous maps about personal, interpersonal, organizational, and social decisions just as you did. I grasped only slowly how things worked in the adult world. I saw that world divided into many mysteriously different compartments, mainly along subject-matter lines, incorporating many different approaches. Talk about complexity and difficulty!"

"Consider," he went on, "how easy it would be for young children to learn about the absolute, action-comparative, responsive, goal-directed, and originative patterns. That's only structuring the difference between choosing on the basis of what you enjoy, or what you prefer, or what you are expected to do, or what you need to do to accomplish something, or what may work out best

# Commentary 10

in the longer run. Children haven't had a lifetime of splitting actions from consequences, so a term like 'alternaquence' shouldn't twist them into knots. From these beginnings, the rest of the decisional structures would come easily, and by the seventh or eighth grade they would have covered them all, allocative, recursive, propositional, organizational, including functionarial, and so on. They would see things whole in a way we simply can't. Imagine what such children might dream up about reorganizing society. It makes me feel positively backward."

"The complexity of a theory," he added, "depends on how many things it assumes. Mine assumes few, but explains a lot, so it's far simpler than the bookshelves of partial and contradictory explanations otherwise needed. The difficulty of learning any new and powerful approach stems mostly from clearing away messy but habitual and linguistically comfortable explanations. Your difficulty and mine do not mean the theory is complex, but only that we have been mistrained."

I find it hard to imagine how a young child might respond to MacNeal's theories, but I report his view. The future might prove him right.

This installment fittingly concludes *Et cetera*'s series on the *Master Atlas* with semantic aspects. They show that to the time-honored distinction between denotation and connotation we must now add demaplication, decision-making implication. Without knowing it, we have been signaling our decisional approaches all along in how we express ourselves. Like body language, demaplication tells things about the speaker that even the speaker may not know. Look out, fellow adults!

The four appendices constituting this tenth and final installment of *MacNeal's Master Atlas* are:
1. At the Demalogical Helm (a textual explication)
2. Sample Demalogical Dictionary Entries
3. Demalogical Thesaurus (greatly abbreviated)
4. Sources (more than a bibliography)

## C. At the demalogical helm *(a textual explication)*

Sea creatures, so we are told, sense ocean currents, salinity, and temperature in negotiating their world, even without being aware of water as such. So, too, do we humans continually navigate fast shifting verbal demalogics without consciously attending to either language or decision making.

To slow such rapid adjustments to visible speed we can take a frozen text and attempt to spell out its demalogical implications. But we must be careful to use an old text, or at least one not too close to any immediate decision, so that we can hold fast long enough to look beneath the surface.

The passage I have chosen was written more than 2,400 years ago by the great historian Thucydides. It concerns a delegation from Corcyra that had come around Greece from its northwestern island to ask Athens for help in fighting Corinth. In the words of the Crawley translation: "An assembly was convoked ... and the Corcyraeans spoke as follows:" [numbers in brackets refer to my demalogical explication]

'[1]Athenians! [2]when [3]a [4]people that [5]have not [6]rendered any [7]important [8]service or [9]support to [10]their [11]neighbours in [12]times past, [13]for which [14]they might [15]claim to be [16]repaid, [17]appear before [18]them as [19]we now [20]appear before [21]you [22]to [23]solicit [24]their [25]assistance, [26]they may [27]fairly [28]be required [29]to satisfy [30]certain preliminary conditions. [31]They [32]should show, [33]first, that [34]it is [35]expedient [36]or [37]at least safe to [38]grant [39]their [40]request; [41]next, that [42]they [43]will retain a lasting sense of the kindness. But if they cannot clearly establish any of these points, they must not be annoyed if they meet with a rebuff. Now the Corcyraeans believe that with their petition for assistance they can also give you a satisfactory answer on these points, and they have therefore despatched us hither. It has so happened that our [past] policy as regards you, with respect to this request, turns out to be inconsistent, and as regards our interests, to be at the present crisis inexpedient. We say inconsistent, because a power which has never in the whole of her past history been willing to ally herself with any of her neighbours, is now found asking them to ally themselves with her. And we say inexpedient, because in our present war with

Corinth it has left us in a position of entire isolation, and what once seemed the wise precaution of refusing to involve ourselves in alliances with other powers, lest we should also involve ourselves in risks of their choosing, has now proved to be folly and weakness. ... '

A Demalogical Explication

1. "Athenians," not just persons, but citizens of Athens, invokes organizational and demasystems demalogics and requests a functionarial ear for the proposal to come
2. "when" introduces a situation in the responsive pattern
3. "a" marks the upcoming situation as part of a generalized rule
4. "people" brings in a reinforcing organizational and demasystems reference
5. "have not" places the act in the past and emphasizes that it is the situational part of a responsive pattern
6. "rendered" marks a particularly responsive form of giving; it implies a giving back
7. "important" raises the possibility of a scorecard approach in which some factors will be weighted more than others
8. "service" implies an act that begs responsive reciprocity
9. "support" also begs responsive reciprocity, and especially in favoring one party over another, just the kind of help the Corcyraeans now seek
10. "their" invokes belonging ("ownership") and responsive expectations
11. "neighbours" is both responsive and reciprocal; neighbors are expected to treat each other in certain ways
12. "times past" again emphasizes a situation; anything past is situation
13. "for which" reflects responsive and reciprocal demalogic
14. "they" refers to a proposer
15. "claim" identifies a proposal with strong responsive support
16. "repaid" raises again both responsive and reciprocal demalogics
17. "appear before" reflects propositional demalogic
18. "them" identifies the deciders to whom the proposal is addressed
19. "we" identifies the current proposer
20. "appear before" again reflects propositional demalogic
21. "you" identifies the deciders to whom the current proposal is addressed
22. "to" introduces goal-directed demalogic; in order to
23. "solicit" labels a kind of proposing
24. "their" refers again to the deciders to whom the proposal is addressed
25. "assistance" suggests mutual demalogic, a doing together
26. "they" refers to the proposers
27. "fairly" is a responsive judgment on what is fitting
28. "be required" begins to define what is fitting
29. "to satisfy" introduces a goal to be fulfilled
30. "certain preliminary conditions" further defines the goal, which is also seen in responsive terms as the situation that must be present before going further, a precondition

31. "They" refers to the proposers
32. "should" represents a judgment within the combined goal-directed and responsive frameworks (I almost said "frame words") now set up
33. "first" signals a compound pattern
34. "it is" introduces a situation, here a further definition of "preliminary conditions"
35. "expedient" most likely refers to an action that would be advantageous in the originative or scorecard sense (and clearly not to what is right in a responsive sense); an appeal to immediate practicality
36. "or" shows the Corcyraean delegation about to propose an alternate demalogic to the Athenians
37. "at least safe" states the goal (safety) as a minimum condition, thereby probably part of a compound (likely a scorecard) pattern
38. "grant" refers to the response of a decider to a proposal
39. "their" refers once again to the proposer
40. "request" refers to the action proposed, reemphasizing propositional demalogic
41. "next" again signals multiple reasons within a compound pattern
42. "they" refers once again to the proposer
43. "will retain" classifies a future event (retaining) as part of the "preliminary conditions," which raises a reasonable question of whether it should properly be classified as a situation (sure thing) or an alternaquence (unsure thing)

. . .

That's enough. You finish it, if you want. It just seems to take forever spelling out the obvious in absurd detail with big words.

The main point of this explication is to show how fast we humans handle shifting demalogics, what plodders we would be otherwise. Like Joe DiMaggio in center field, we make it look easy. That ease obscures our skill. Try a computer on demalogical complications and it may mess up, as in the famous story of translating "the spirit indeed is willing, but the flesh is weak" (Matthew 26:41) into Russian as "the vodka is really strong but the meat is putrid." (There's a fast farewell to goal-directed-and-absolute-pattern conflict.) Perhaps comparative demalogics will help computers translate better, and maybe even someday make more complicated demalogical discriminations and adjustments. But in the meanwhile we plain machineless humans can walk surprisingly tall.

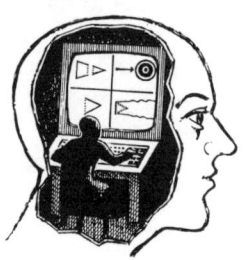

# D. Sample demalogical-dictionary entries

The few terms defined here illustrate the variety and richness of demalogical implication. The first (unnumbered) definition for each term has been selected from the alternatives in a Merriam-Webster New Collegiate Dictionary. The other definitions carry a number for each demalogical implication of the first definition. The terms are not presented alphabetically, but more or less in sequence from simpler to more complex demalogics. Most of these terms are multidemalogical. One of them, "competent," is omnidemalogical.

**birthday** *n* : an anniversary of one's birth **1***responsive*: an occasion to observe with a present or friendly comment to the one whose birthday it is

**need** *n* : a lack of something requisite **1***goal-directed*: a lack of means to achieve a goal

**waste** *vt* : to use carelessly **1***allocative*: to reduce one's options more than necessary or worthwhile

**double cross** *n* : an act of betraying or cheating an associate **1***recursive*+**2***responsive*+**3***mutual* or **4***reciprocal*: an act contrary to an agreement with a second decider, which agreement called for action contrary to a separate agreement with a third decider

**married** *adj* : being in the state of matrimony **1***responsive*: not available, already taken **2***organizational*+**3***enfounding*: having participated in creating a new demaunit (married couple, family) **4***functionarial*: able to speak as a functionary of that demaunit **5***mutual*+**6***reciprocal*: used to the give and take of interpersonal relations

**teach** *vt* : to cause to know how **1***propositional*: to offer knowledge to another **2***goal-directed*: to try to make another know how **3***allocative*: to increase another decider's options

**teacher** *n* : one whose occupation is to instruct **1***organizational*+**2***functionarial*: one who teaches, esp. as a staff member of a school or other organization **3**unknown *basic* or *compound demapattern* : one who chooses to teach (hence the query "how did you get into teaching?") **4***propositional*, **5***goal-directed*, and **6***allocative*—see **teach**

**teachers college** *n* : a college for the training of teachers **1***organizational*+**2***recursive*: an organization offering courses of instruction, including ones teaching how to teach **3***enstaffing*: a school increasing the pool of persons available as teachers **4***propositional*+**5***goal-directed*+**6***allocative*—see **teach** **7***functionarial* and **8**unknown *basic* or *compound demapattern*—see **teacher**

**cartel** *n* : a combination of independent commercial enterprises designed to limit competition **1***organizational*+**2***enfounding*+**3***second-order*+**4***functionarial*+**5***mutual*+**6***goal-directed*+**7***allocative*: an organization founded by the staff of otherwise independent commercial organizations to cooperate in reducing competition and thereby controlling the offerings to customers, etc.

**competent** *adj* : having requisite ability **1***absolute*: able to tell what one likes and dislikes **2***action-comparative*: able to tell what one prefers **3***responsive*: able to respond appropriately **4***goal-directed*: able to direct one's actions toward desired results **5***originative*: able to choose directly between alternaquences **6***uniform*: able to employ concurring reasons in the same pattern **7***multiform*: able to employ concurring reasons in different patterns **8***scorecard*: able to weigh factors for and against a choice **9***sequential*: able to follow a stepwise procedure employing different patterns at each step **10***transformative*: able to restate reasons in other patterns **11***quantitative*: able to put decisions into numerical terms **12***recursive*: able to make decisions about decisions **13***allocative*: able to anticipate how an action might affect the availability of other actions **14***propositional*: able to propose available courses of action to others **15***mutual*: able to act in concert with others taking like actions not otherwise available **16***reciprocal*: able to take action in exchange for a different action by another decider **17***enfounding*: able to create and disband extrahuman demaunits **18***enstaffing*: able to engage and disengage personnel for an extrahuman demaunit **19***functionarial*: able to function as the staff of an organization **20***second-order*: able functionarially to enfound or enstaff another extrahuman demaunit **21***demasystem*: able to use a system of recursive functionarial responsive decisions about responsive functionarial decisions **22***comparative demalogics*: able to compare demalogics **23**able to use various combinations of the foregoing demalogics

**work** *n* : activity in which one exerts strength or faculties to do or perform something **a:** sustained physical or mental effort to overcome obstacles and achieve an objective or result **b:** the labor, task, or duty that affords one his [sic] accustomed means of livelihood **c:** a specific task, duty, function, or assignment often being a part or phase of some larger activity **1***absolute*: drudgery **2***responsive*: duty, chore **3***goal-directed*: effort as means to an end **4***originative*: what one does (one's life*work*) **5***sequential*: a demanding step in a larger sequence (now comes the [real] work) **6***allocative*: preparation for other actions coming later **7***functionarial*: actions performed in an organizational capacity **8**various combinations of the foregoing demalogics

· · ·

Note how the three-part Websterian definition of "work" conveys some of the variation specified in the eight demalogical definitions. This points up an interesting linguistic speculation. Could demalogical perspectives be a prime source for variation in meanings? If so, such variations in meaning would result not from different experience, as usually assumed, but from an application of our common inheritance of multiple demalogical perspectives.

Then look at "cartel," whose meaning involves a specific complex of mostly learned demalogics. Doesn't this complex, and not just lack of experience, help shield the term's meaning from the young and also from semantic shift?

# E. Demalogical thesaurus *(abridged)*

The demalogical thesaurus that follows has been abridged for *Et cetera* at the request of its editors. It differs from the original and from usual thesaurus construction in the following significant respects:
1. It lacks an opening synopsis of categories. (It does, however, follow a regular demalogical progression, so that all categories in the 100 series fall on structural level 1, subdecisional events, all in the 200 series fall on level 2, basic patterns, and so on.)
2. There is no index. (If there were, it would have a disproportionate number of entries from the beginning of the alphabet, because of the abridgment.)
3. The number of entries has been held roughly equal for each category. (This underrepresents such highly verbalized categories as the responsive, goal-directed, allocative, and propositional far more than such less verbalized ones as the originative and recursive.)

This thesaurus began as lists of key words in my earlier and still unpublished 1982 work on demalogics, which I now refer to, in honor of its bulk, as "The Too Complete Decider." That effort resulted in about 900 entries. In 1984 I started adding more terms as part of a computerized investigation into the frequency of demalogical terms. That raised total entries past 1,500 by February 1987. I have since added terms primarily for my own writing convenience. (Don't laugh. Dr. Peter Mark Roget began his compilation for his own convenience.) The total now stands at nearly 4,000 entries. A modest effort could raise it to 10,000. I believe that a complete demalogical thesaurus of the English language would then be in reach, but only for professional demalogical lexicographers, presently an unoccupied occupation.

You may wonder why a demalogical thesaurus is needed; won't an ordinary thesaurus do? The answer is no, it won't. Before you get the wrong idea or think I am ungrateful, let me tell you that I love both well-worn copies of my ordinary thesaurus and greatly respect all those who ever worked on it.

The editor (Robert L. Chapman) of my fourth edition *Roget's International Thesaurus* states that it "collects great semantic 'domains' under large conceptual headings, and shows by the manner of organization the tracks the mind may take as it ranges about in a given territory." The editor and the publishers (New York, Crowell; London and Sydney, Harper & Row) "believe that the new edition ... constitutes the most elaborate approach yet made to the specification of possible concepts." It is in their words "the best empirical base for research in structural semantics...."

I am forced to agree, because we don't yet have a full demalogical thesaurus. Indeed, in years past, compiling a dictionary that defined, or a thesaurus that organized, terms by their decisional implications was out of the question. The task requires both computer power and a demalogical framework.

Whoever now compiles such a dictionary and thesaurus will, in my judgment, open up startling new capabilities in machine translation and analysis. I, for one, would love to know how the relative frequency of demalogics has varied over the centuries, and how it now varies by profession, religion, political organization, and so forth. Do educators now stress responsive demalogic less than when I was in school and goal-directed demalogic more, and has this affected students? Are environmentalists more originative than industrialists or do they just emphasize different goals? I have a hundred such questions and more that demalogical analysis could answer.

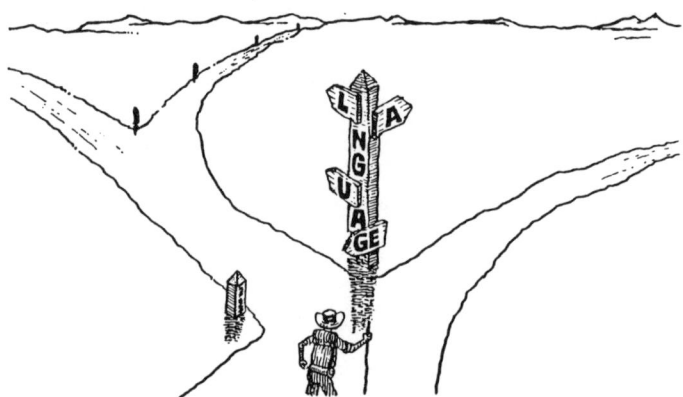

I could also reduce the wear on my Rogets caused by the incessant flipping back and forth as I search for terms in specific demalogics that now lie scattered about. As you know, a thesaurus does not define terms; rather, it brings together in one place terms that are synonyms, antonyms, or likely to be used in the same context. Roget's thesaurus does not perform this function for demalogical use. Its organizational scheme (apparently little changed since 1805) quite understandably ignores, separates similar, and juxtaposes dissimilar, demalogics.

**LEVEL ONE: Subdecisional Events**
**A. Event in General**
      100. HAPPENING
  NOUNS: **happening**, development, event, occurrence, phenomenon
  VERBS: **happen**, come to pass, develop, occur, take place, transpire
  ADJS: **actual**, at hand, coming, happened, happening, real
  OTHER: **really**, actually, in fact
**B. Situation**
      110. UNALTERABLE CIRCUMSTANCE
  NOUNS: **fact**, certainty, circumstance, situation, way it is

  VERBS: **is**, has been, exists, set, bound to happen, will be
  ADJS: **given**, certain, done, inevitable, past, spilt milk, unavoidable
  OTHER: **actually**, in any event, inevitably, really, unavoidably
**C. Alternaquence**
      120. ALTERNAQUENCE
  NOUNS: **alternaquence**, choice, course, option, path, scenario, way
  VERBS: **diverge**, pick one's road
  ADJS: **alternaquential**, divergent
  OTHER: **alternaquentially**, divergently, on the other hand, or

# Demalogical thesaurus

**D. Action**

121. ACTION
NOUNS: **action**, act, alternative, choice, course, deed, doing
VERBS: **do**, act, make happen
ADJS: **doing**, by choice, doable
OTHER: **actively**, in action

**E. Consequence**

122. CONSEQUENCE
NOUNS: **consequence**, aftermath, effect, outcome, result, what follows
VERBS: **follow**, develop, ensue; **cause**, generate, originate, produce
ADJS: **resulting**, ensuing, produced
OTHER: **consequently**, as a result, because, hence

BASIC PATTERNS

**LEVEL TWO: Basic Demapatterns**
**A. Basic Pattern in General**

200. ONE REASON FOR ONE ACTION
NOUNS: **the reason**, only reason, open-and-shut case, simple choice
VERBS: **pick**, choose, decide, elect, select; **reject**, spurn, turn down
ADJS: **simple**, automatic, clear-cut, direct, obvious, straightforward
OTHER: **simply**, automatically, obviously, of course, plainly

**B. Absolute Pattern**

210. TASTE IN GENERAL
NOUNS: **taste**, feeling, sensation
VERBS: **taste**, feel, sense
ADJS: **sensitive**, tasteful
OTHER: **sensuously**, sensitively, tastefully

211. LIKING
NOUNS: **liking**, delight, enjoyment, fun, joy, treat
VERBS: **like**, adore, eat up, enjoy, love, relish; **please**, charm, delight
ADJS: **likeable**, delicious, delightful, good, pleasant
OTHER: **likeably**, fondly, joyously

212. DISLIKING
NOUNS: **disliking**, aversion, dislike, distaste, pain, repugnance
VERBS: **dislike**, detest, hate, loath
ADJS: **unlikeable**, abominable, bad-tasting, disgusting, disliked, dull
OTHER: **unpleasantly**, painfully

**C. Action-Comparative Pattern**

220. ACTION COMPARISON
NOUNS: **preference**, choice, favorite
VERBS: **prefer**, favor, take before
ADJS: **preferable**, better, more to my taste
OTHER: **preferably**, instead, rather

**D. Responsive Pattern**

230. RESPONSIVENESS
NOUNS: **responsiveness**, response, reaction; **unresponsiveness**, apathy
VERBS: **respond**, react, reply
ADJS: **responsive**, answering, reactive; **unresponsive**, unreactive, inert
OTHER: **responsively**, habitually

231. SITUATION
NOUNS: **situation**, circumstance, condition; **obligation**, agreement; **time & place**, birthday, church; **type of person**, boss, child; **property**, possession; **customary thing**, poison ivy; **precondition**, requirement
VERBS: **trigger**, bring up, create a situation, set off
ADJS: **conditioned**, asleep, busy, deserving, drunk, guilty, her, his
OTHER: **conditionally**, always, as soon as, if, in the event of, never

232. RESPONSE
NOUNS: **response**, reaction, reply; **custom**, revenge, thanks
VERBS: **respond**, answer, react; **appreciate**; **not respond**; **dishonor**
ADJS: **responsive**, replying;

**appreciative**, grateful, sorry
OTHER: **responsively**, in reply; **asleep at the switch**

### 233. RULE
NOUNS: **rule**, convention, custom, expectation, law
VERBS: **expect**, deem, predicate, prejudge, presume, rule
ADJS: **customary**, expected
OTHER: **customarily**, called for, presumably

### 234. RESPONSIVE JUDGMENT
NOUNS: **responsiveness**, consistency, dependability; **disregard**, sin
VERBS: **behave**, be good, do right; **misbehave**, act up, cheat; **should**
ADJS: **appropriate**, fitting, just, right; **inappropriate**, unfair, wrong
OTHER: **appropriately**, fairly, properly; **inappropriately**, unjustly

## E. Goal-Directed Pattern

### 240. GOAL-DIRECTEDNESS
NOUNS: **goal-directedness**, intent, intention, purpose
VERBS: **intend**, aspire, mean
ADJS: **goal-directed**, intentional, purposive
OTHER: **purposely**, intentionally, on purpose

### 241. PURPOSE
NOUNS: **goal**, aim; **need**, deficiency; **desire**, ambition; **plan**, blueprint; **problem**, barrier; **effort**, attempt; **specific goals:** approval, beauty
VERBS: **want**, desire; **design**, arrange; **carry out**, execute
ADJS: **targeted**; **ambitious**; **needed**; **planned**; **troublesome**
OTHER: **for**, in order to, to

### 242. MEANS
NOUNS: **means**, way; **tool**, lever; **resource**, input; **helper**, aid
VERBS: **use; ask; argue; attack; compete; cultivate; find; fix; guard; hunt; instruct; maintain; make; send**

ADJS: **useful**, instrumental, used
OTHER: **usefully**, how, somehow, thus

### 243. GOAL-DIRECTED JUDGMENT
NOUNS: **purposefulness; success; aimlessness; failure; side effect**
VERBS: **achieve**, complete, succeed, win; **fail**, flunk, lose, quit
ADJS: **successful**, achieved, effective; **unsuccessful**, abortive, failed
OTHER: **successfully; unsuccessfully**

## F. Originative Pattern

### 250. ORIGINATIVENESS
NOUNS: **origination**, fountainhead, generation, generator, origin, source
VERBS: **originate**, generate, start
ADJS: **originative**, generative, original, originating, starting
OTHER: **originatively**, as you sow, ye are like to reap

### 251. ALTERNAQUENCES
NOUNS: **alternaquences**, alternatives, different paths, options, scenarios
VERBS: **diverge**, choose a path, commit, decide between
ADJS: **alternaquential**, divergent
OTHER: **alternaquentially**, divergently, the die is cast

### 252. PREFERENCE
NOUNS: **preference**, bent, inclination
VERBS: **prefer**, favor, incline to
ADJS: **preferred**, favored; **inclined**
OTHER: **preferably**, rather

### 253. WHOLENESS
NOUNS: **wholeness**, holism, non-elementalism, whole
VERBS: **consider as wholes**, include, take all in all
ADJS: **overall**, holistic, non-elementalistic, whole
OTHER: **on the whole**, all in all, altogether, as a unit, inclusively

# Demalogical thesaurus

LEVEL THREE: Compound Demapatterns
## A. Compound Pattern in General

300. COMPOUNDEDNESS IN GENERAL
NOUNS: **criteria**, another side, complication, grounds, reasons, values
VERBS: **have reasons**, complicate, compound, give reasons
ADJS: **complex**, complicated, compounded, many-sided, not simple
OTHER: **besides**, and, another reason, but, further, in addition

301. COMPOUNDS BY BASIC PATTERN
NOUNS: **likes**, dislikes; **preferences**, favorites; **rules**; **goals**, aims

## B. Uniform Pattern

310. UNIFORM PATTERN
NOUNS: **duplication**, confirmation
VERBS: **double**, confirm, kill two birds with one stone
ADJS: **manifold**, compatible, multiple
OTHER: **similarly**, in the same vein

## C. Multiform Pattern

320. MULTIFORM PATTERN
NOUNS: **heterogeneity**, mixture, multiformity
VERBS: **mix**, cover all the bases
ADJS: **multiform**, divergent, diverse
OTHER: **diversely**, oddly, variously

## D. Scorecard Pattern

330. SCORECARDNESS IN GENERAL
NOUNS: **weighing**, score; **opposing reasons**, aspects, counterindications
VERBS: **disagree**, break up, divide, fragment, oppose, side
ADJS: **opposing**, balanced, piecemeal
OTHER: **contrarily**, piece by piece

331. PROS & CONS
NOUNS: **pros & cons**, advantages & disdvantages, pluses & minuses
VERBS: **balance**, compensate for, counterbalance, equalize, offset
ADJS: **opposing**, balanced, contradictory, offsetting, positive & negative
OTHER: **for & against**, contradictorily, on the other hand

332. UNPAIRED FEATURE
NOUNS: **feature**, argument, catch, clincher, contention, drawback
VERBS: **distinguish**, contrast, not compare with, stand apart, unbalance
ADJS: **unmatched**, incomparable, peerless, separate, unbalanced, unique
OTHER: **differently**, although, but, however, though, yet

333. VALUE CONFLICT
NOUNS: **opposition**, conflict, contradiction, disagreement, dispute
VERBS: **conflict**, contradict, disagree, negate, oppose
ADJS: **conflicting**, opposing
OTHER: **versus**, against, contrary to, on the other hand, yes but

334. WEIGHING (SCORING)
NOUNS: **weighing**, benefit, cost, importance, scorecard, significance
VERBS: **weigh**, analyze, balance, calculate, evaluate, judge, score
ADJS: **calculable**, important, relative, significant
OTHER: **as against**, compared to, relatively, versus

335. OVERRIDING REASON
NOUNS: **decisive factor**, crux, heart of the matter, main point, real issue
VERBS: **override**, control, dominate, prevail, really count, swamp
ADJS: **paramount**, conclusive, controlling, critical, decisive
OTHER: **although**, anyway, despite, even so, however, nevertheless

336. SUMMARY JUDGMENT
NOUNS: **bottom line**, net benefit,

net value, preponderance, score
VERBS: **outweigh**, come down on the side of, outbalance, outscore
ADJS: **net**, balanced, final, indeterminate, outweighed, summary
OTHER: **in the end**, in the final analysis, when push comes to shove

### E. Sequential Patterns

340. SEQUENCING IN GENERAL
NOUNS: **sequence**, order, progression, series, step
VERBS: **take it in steps**, come next, put in some order, sequence
ADJS: **sequential**, progressive, step-by-step
OTHER: **sequentially**, first things first, in turn, step by step

341. ELABORATION
NOUNS: **elaboration**, amplification, details, small strokes
VERBS: **elaborate**, add details, amplify, detail, develop, flesh out
ADJS: **elaborated**, detailed, developed, worked out in detail
OTHER: **to completion**, from the top down, in detail

342. TESTING
NOUNS: **test**, review, round robin
VERBS: **test**, review, try, try on
ADJS: **tested**, reviewed
OTHER: **after testing**, on review, from all angles

**LEVEL FOUR: Basic Demalinkages**

### A. Linkage in General

400. LINKAGE IN GENERAL
NOUNS: **linkage**, connection, interconnection, juncture, link, relation

VERBS: **link**, affect, connect, interconnect, interrelate, relate
ADJS: **linked**, affected by, connected, interconnected, related
OTHER: **interconnectedly**, in connection with

### B. Transformative Linkage

410. TRANSFORMATION
NOUNS: **transformation**, change, excuse, rationalization, story
VERBS: **transform**, alter, change story, rationalize, revise
ADJS: **transformative**, altered, changed, interpreted, revised
OTHER: **put another way**, in a new version, in other words

### C. Quantitative Linkage

420. QUANTITATIVENESS
NOUNS: **quantity**, calculation, count, number, percentage, statistic; **quantitative fields:** accounting, banking, engineering, game theory
VERBS: **quantify**, calculate, count, measure, number, scale
ADJS: **quantitative**, numerical, optimal, statistical
OTHER: **quantitatively**, numerically, statistically

### D. Recursive Linkage

430. RECURSION
NOUNS: **recursion**, feedback, recursiveness, self-reflexiveness
VERBS: **refer to itself**, apply to itself, reflect, turn back on
ADJS: **recursive**, circular, self-reflexive, self-regulating
OTHER: **recursively**, on itself, self-reflexively, to itself

### E. Allocative Linkage

440. ALLOCATION IN GENERAL
NOUNS: **allocation**, allowance, budget, distribution, division
VERBS: **allocate**, affect, allot, allow, commit, distribute
ADJS: **allocative**, affected, allocable, allowed, scheduled
OTHER: **allocatively**, save for a rainy day, timely

### 441. EXPANSION OF CHOICE
NOUNS: **facilitation**, development, education, learning how, shopping
VERBS: **enable**, accumulate, acquire, add to your choices, cultivate
ADJS: **enabling**, creative, cultivated, free, learned, new
OTHER: **more easily**, a stitch in time saves nine, creatively, economically

### 442. REDUCTION OF CHOICE
NOUNS: **disablement**, consumption, cost, damage, death, decay, loss
VERBS: **weaken**, blind, block, break, clip the wings of, contaminate
ADJS: **disabling**, broken, dead, disorganized, dissipated, dropped
OTHER: **wastefully**, extravagantly, inefficiently, out of

### 443. RESOURCE
NOUNS: **resource**, ability, asset, cash flow, crop, energy, equipment
VERBS: **reserve**, conserve, economize, handle, maintain, save up
ADJS: **reserved**, accumulated, allocatable, available, flexible
OTHER: **on hand**, in hand, in reserve, in store, under control

INTERPERSONAL LINKAGES

**LEVEL FIVE: Interpersonal Demalinkages**
## A. Interpersonal Linkage in General

### 500. INTERPERSONALNESS IN GENERAL
NOUNS: **communication**, communicativeness, give-and-take, interaction
VERBS: **communicate**, debate, exchange ideas, interact
ADJS: **communicated**, communicable, debated, interactive
OTHER: **interpersonally**, between you and me, communally, conversationally

## B. Propositional Linkage

### 510. PROPOSAL
NOUNS: **proposal**, advice, bid, command, demand, notice, offer
VERBS: **propose**, admonish, advance, advise, alert, apply, ask, beg, bid
ADJS: **propositional**, demanding, influential, insistent, inviting
OTHER: **propositionally**, insistently, invitingly, please, will you

### 511. RESPONSE TO PROPOSAL
NOUNS: **response**, acceptance, answer, consent, counterproposal, decision
VERBS: **respond**, accept, agree, answer, consider, decide, decline
ADJS: **responding**, accepted, agreed, answering, approved, consenting
OTHER: **in response**, in answer, in reply, unwillingly, willingly

## C. Mutual Linkage

### 520. MUTUALITY
NOUNS: **mutuality**, conference, joining, participation, togetherness
VERBS: **join**, come together, get together, meet, participate
ADJS: **mutual**, joined, joint, married, our, unanimous
OTHER: **mutually**, jointly, side by side, together, with; **we**, us

### 521. COOPERATION
NOUNS: **cooperation**, alliance, assistance, coalition, collaboration
VERBS: **cooperate**, assist, collaborate, join together, join with
ADJS: **cooperative**, allied, collaborative, cooperating, mutual
OTHER: **cooperatively**, conjointly, in partnership, together, with

### 522. CONFLICT
NOUNS: **conflict**, argument, battle,

combat, dispute, duel, fight
VERBS: **fight**, argue, challenge, compete, dispute, duel, join in battle
ADJS: **conflicting**, argumentative, competing, embattled, quarrelsome
OTHER: **against**, at war, competitively, in opposition to, versus

### D. Reciprocal Linkage

530. RECIPROCITY IN GENERAL

NOUNS: **reciprocity**, compensation, contract, deal, exchange
VERBS: **reciprocate**, compensate, complement, deal, do each other favors
ADJS: **reciprocal**, complementary, exchangeable, repayable
OTHER: **reciprocally**, complementarily, in exchange, vice versa

531. ECONOMIC EXCHANGE

NOUNS: **commerce**, bargaining, business, buying, economics, marketing
VERBS: **trade**, auction, barter, bid, buy, deal, discount, do business
ADJS: **commercial**, bought, business, economic, marketed, monetary, paid
OTHER: **commercially**, economically, for sale, monetarily, to rent

### E. Organizational Linkages

540. ORGANIZATION IN GENERAL

NOUNS: **organization**, army, association, business, chapter, church
VERBS: **organize**, administer, staff
ADJS: **organizational**, academic, business, corporate, departmental
OTHER: **organizationally**, corporately, departmentally, governmentally

550. ENFOUNDING

NOUNS: **enfounding**, creation, establishment; **dissolution**, breakup, end
VERBS: **enfound**, assemble, charter, found; **dissolve**, break up, close
ADJS: **enfounded**, founded, organized; **liquidated**, closed
OTHER: **organizationally**, at the end

560. ENSTAFFING

NOUNS: **enstaffing**, appointment, delegation, election; **dismissal**
VERBS: **enstaff**, appoint, commission, delegate, elect, employ; **discharge**
ADJS: **appointed**, commissioned, delegated, elected; **fired**, defrocked
OTHER: **by appointment**, help wanted

570. FUNCTIONARIALNESS

NOUNS: **functionary**, administrator, attaché,, boss, captain, chairman
VERBS: **function**, act, attend to business, carry out, conduct
ADJS: **functionarial**, acting, businesslike, executive, official
OTHER: **functionarially**, officially, on behalf of, professionally

580. SECOND-ORDER LINKAGE

NOUNS: **administration**, management; **alliance**, cartel; **rules**, bylaws
VERBS: **administer**, manage; **affiliate**, amalgamate; **codify**
ADJS: **administrative**, federal, governing, regulatory
OTHER: **administratively**, federally, internationally, managerially

**LEVEL SIX: Demasystems**

### A. Demasystems

600. DEMASYSTEMIZATION

NOUNS: **demasystem**, civilization, culture, rule of law, society
VERBS: **systematize**, civilize, methodize, normalize, organize, regulate
ADJS: **systematized**, civilized, systematic, well-regulated
OTHER: **systematically**, by regulation, governmentally, methodically

### 601. RULES
NOUNS: **rules**, laws; **codification**, amendment; **legal procedure**
VERBS: **codify**, amend, enact, legalize, legislate, make law, prohibit
ADJS: **legal**, actionable, customary, legislative, normal, statutory
OTHER: **legally**, constitutionally, ethically, lawfully

### 602. SYSTEM FUNCTIONARY
NOUNS: **official**, attorney, bailiff, commissioner, deputy, guardian
VERBS: **officiate**, conduct, do one's duty, execute, function, judge
ADJS: **official**, bureaucratic, duly constituted, judicial, legal
OTHER: **officially**, bureaucratically, by authority of, judicially, legally

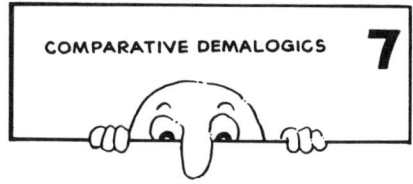

## LEVEL SEVEN: Comparative Demalogics
### A. Awareness

### 700. AWARENESS
NOUNS: **awareness**, deliberation, demaconsciousness, post mortem
VERBS: **debate**, argue, consider, decide consciously, deliberate
ADJS: **aware**, deliberate, demaconscious, wide awake
OTHER: **deliberately**, consciously, demaconsciously

### 701. SEMANTICS
NOUNS: **meaning**, relevance, significance; **multidemalogical terms: decision; proposal; explanation; motivation; responsibility; error; competence; intelligence; play; work; humor; beauty; value; issue**
VERBS: **explicate**, analyze, explain
ADJS: **meaningful**, demalogical, multidemalogical, relevant, semantic
OTHER: **semantically**, demalogically, linguistically, of significance

### 702. DEMATHEORY
NOUNS: **dematheory**, comparative demalogics, pattern, linkage

### B. Persuasion

### 710. SCHOOL
NOUNS: **persuasion**, belief; **school: animism; behaviorism; determinism**
VERBS: **believe**, accept, assume; **politicize; psychologize**
ADJS: **persuasive**, believing; **fatalistic; hedonistic; scientific**
OTHER: **believingly**, in one's opinion; **psychologically; scientifically**

### 711. FOCUS
NOUNS: **focus**, dematype, outlook, perspective, point of view, style
VERBS: **focus**, direct attention to, emphasize
ADJS: **dematypical**, absolute, action-comparative, allocative
OTHERS: **dematypically**, allocatively, as I see it, originatively

### C. Responsibility

### 720. RESPONSIBILITY
NOUNS: **responsibility**, accountability, conscientiousness, dependability
VERBS: **take responsibility**, be accountable, be irresponsible
ADJS: **responsible**, accountable, conscientious, consistent, dependable
OTHER: **responsibly**, conscientiously, dependably, dishonorably

### 721. ERROR
NOUNS: **error**, accident, blunder
VERBS: **make a mistake**, blunder, err, forget, ignore, overlook
ADJS: **erroneous**, bad, forgetful, ignorant, mistaken, wrong
OTHER: **erroneously**, foolishly, forgetfully, mistakenly, wrongly

### 722. ANTICIPATION
NOUNS: **anticipation**, estimate, expectation, forecast
VERBS: **anticipate**, estimate, expect, forecast, foresee, guess
ADJS: **forecast**, estimated, expected
OTHER: **likely**, expectedly, probably

## D. Action Orientation

### 730. PRACTICE

NOUNS: **practice**, exercise, fiction, fun, literature, myth, play

VERBS: **practice**, act out, dramatize, enact, play, stage

ADJS: **instructive**, anecdotal, dramatic, editorial, enlightening

OTHER: **educationally**, as an exercise, editorially, for fun

### 731. ACTION

NOUNS: **action**, doer, doing, go-getter; **inaction**, constraint, delay

VERBS: **act**, do, make happen; **hang back**, balk, block, hesitate, stall

ADJS: **active**, able, decisive, resolute; **passive**, indecisive, irresolute

OTHER: **actively**, I, I'll, master of my fate; **passively**, fatalistically, somebody should, they ought to

# F. Sources

Although I would dearly love to cite prestigious sources as the direct antecedents of the *Master Atlas*, I cannot. When I began my demalogical work in earnest in 1947, almost nothing had been written on the subject as such.

I remember the occasion but not the exact date in 1947 when the responsive, goal-directed, and originative patterns all first struck me plain. I also remember the exact moment the next day when I realized that they were *decision-making* patterns.

The progenitors were really my parents, whose sharply divergent styles on practically everything, or so it seemed, led me soon to wonder how each operated. It was perhaps inevitable that my sensitivity to decisional style helped me notice still other styles away from home.

Whether this preparation would have led to the *Master Atlas* without my training in general semantics I cannot say. That training seems to have added three important ingredients: (1) a better framed consciousness of abstracting, (2) a deeper appreciation of the hidden powers of language, and (3) a further push toward scientifically operational definitions. When it comes to decision making, however, Alfred Korzybski and other early general semanticists hardly mention the subject.

Could you help me find something good to read for an hour until my next train?

I have greatly enjoyed and profited from the works of others. Simon's *Administrative Behavior*, which I read early in 1951 (in self-defensive preparation for a June speech on my own theories), cheered me by its pioneering decisional emphasis. Diesing's *Reason in Society* excited me with its unusual emphasis on five types of decision making. Although originally published in 1962, I did not read it or the other works mentioned below before 1977 when I finally sat down to work out my complete approach.

Raiffa's *Decision Analysis* gave me a wonderfully intelligible introduction to statistical decision trees. Hart's *The Concept of Law*, from which I quote, gave me just the authority I sought to confirm the recursive responsiveness of law. Shackle's *Decision, Order and Time in Human Affairs* delighted me with the first use of the term "originative" I had seen other than my own. I have quoted from Greenwald's *Direct Decision Therapy* at length in the text; he buttressed my belief that we decide more things than we think.

The section of *Toward a General Theory of Action*, Parsons & Shils, editors, that I most enjoyed was Kluckhohn's forty-six pages on "Values and Value-Orientations," because it documented the slipperiness of the terms. Quite a few books I have mentioned elsewhere treated the goal-directed pattern as the only (or only rational) approach to decision making, a view with which I heartily disagree. But *QUID* captured my attention for a different reason: its authors, Jorgensen and Fautsko, recommend their quantitative scorecard pattern be used "whenever you have a decision – and especially a life decision – to make." I don't agree with that view either, of course, but at least it's different. So was the Buddhist approach I read.

Most decision-making books and journal articles I have read (in *Ethics*, *American Sociological Review*, and *Journal of Economic Literature*, among others) offer something useful. But none is written within the same framework as the *Master Atlas*. Many try to say more than can be said comfortably from within the limited demalogics used, even the few articles that recognize variations in explanatory approach. These works are neither my source nor places to direct any but experts in the respective fields.

"Surely," you say, "there must be more than this, something further to explore on the *Master Atlas*'s approach to decision making." If you insist, and who am I to stop you, all I can do for now is direct you to a few other of my own works, which follow:

"When Does Consciousness of Abstracting Matter the Most?" *Et cetera*, Spring 1986.
*Demalogics*, Version 2.0, token edition 1986, (propositions in the style of Wittgenstein's *Tractatus*), 70pp + x.*
"The Flaw," *Et cetera*, Fall 1984.
"Semantics and Decision Making," *Et cetera*, Summer 1983.
*Initial Instruction in How People Make Decisions*, xerograph, 1983, (a programmed-instruction booklet), 62pp + ii.*
*The [Too] Complete Decider*, xerograph, 1982, 576pp. + xxi.*
"Foundations of a Theory of Decision Making," xerograph, June 1951.*

* available only by written application to the author.

# Index

*Italic numerals* identify editor's forewords.

Absolute pattern, 27-29, 43, 64, 106
  dangers in, 82-83, 85
  and demalinkages, 49, 50, 64, 79
  and other demapatterns, 28, 44, 79, 122
  uses of, 27, 79, 96-100
  verbal clues and levers of, 49, 64, 91, 94, 127
  mentioned, *75, 118*
Accident, *25*, 32, 56-59, 100
Actions, 7-8, 19-23, 106
  availability of, 20-22, 51-54, 79-80, 97-98, 127
  in demapatterns, 27-34, 39, 44-46, 79, 106-108
  in basic demalinkages, 49, 51-54, 79, 82, 108-109
  in interpersonal demalinkages, 63-68, 109-110
  *See also* Reasons
Action-comparative pattern, 28-29, 43, 106
  and demalinkages, 49, 50
  and originative pattern, 39
  verbal clues and levers of, 40, 49, 127
  mentioned, *118*
Action-consequence split, 19-20, *119*
  *See also* Elementalism
Action orientation, 96-98
*Administrative Behavior* (Simon), 136
*Admiral of the Ocean Sea* (Morison), 4
Alexander, Jerome, *13*
Allocative demalinkage, 51-55, 109, 112
  dangers in, 53-55, 82-83
  and other demalogics, 71, 74
  quiz on, 72
  uses of, 52-53, 71, 96, *104*
  verbal clues and levers of, 91, 94, 98, 123-25, 130-31
  mentioned, *75, 119*

Alternaquences, 9, *14*, 18-23, 106, 112, *119*
  forecasts of, *76*, 84-85, 100
  in originative pattern, 39-42, 57, 64
  quiz on, 22
  versus situations, *14*, 21-23
  mentioned, 16, 74, 122, 124
Alternative futures, 9
  *See also* Alternaquences
*American Sociological Review*, 136
Argument, 30-31, 56, 120-22
Aristotle, 33
Ashforth, Blake E., *75n*

Basic demapatterns. *See* Demapatterns, basic
Brim, Orville G., Jr., 36
Bureaucracy, *47*, 71-74, *75*
  *See also* Business; Organizational demalinkages
Business, 2, 69, 98
  and demalinkages, 50, 53-55, 58, 74
  and demapatterns, 8, 27, 31, 43, 45, 56-58, 79
  *See also* Organizational demalinkages

Change of mind, 51
  *See also* Recursive demalinkage
Chapman, Robert L., 125
Children, 20, *25*, 45, 66, 70, *118-19*, 124
Columbus, Christopher, 4, 34
Comparative demalogics, 11-12, 16-17, 71, 77-78, 98-100, 111
  in decision making, 12, 77-81, 96-98
  of error, 81-83
  and forecasts, 84-85
  of responsibilities, 86-87, 91-92
  semantic implications of, 120-34
  and social science, *75-76*
  in understanding people, 56-59, 86-87, *89-90*, 92-98
  verbal clues and levers in, 92-95, 120-34

137

Competence, 98, 123-24
Complete decider, 98-99
"The [Too] Complete Decider" (MacNeal), 136
Complexity, *13*, 29, 80, *90*
  of decisions, 80, 98
  demalogical, of terms, 122-24
  of demapatterns, 41-45
  of dematheory, *13-14, 104, 118-19*
  of events, 66
Compound pattern. *See* Demapatterns, compound
*Concept of Law* (Hart), 73, 136
Conference in factory, 55-59
Conflict, *26*, 64, 78, 83
  of behavioral indicators, *26*, 44
  between demapatterns, 41, 56-58, 74, 122
  between demasystems, 74
  resolution of, 41, 45, 57-59, 79-80, 98-100
Confusion, *13*, 41-42, 44-45, *89-90*, 98
Congregational church, 20
*Conscientious Objections* (Postman), 101
Consciousness
  of decisions, 9, 78, 86-87
  of demalogics, *25*, 98, 120, 135
  mentioned, 15, 28, *37*, 100
  *See also* Comparative demalogics
Consequences, 19-23, 106-108, 113, *119*
  and demapatterns, 27-28, 30-36, 39-42, 44, 71, 79
  mentioned, 12, 16, 98
Consistency, 10, 31, 41, 83
Continuity, 6-7, 18-19, 40-41, 74
Contradictions, 30, 41, 45, *119*
Cooperation, 9, 34, 64, 96, 131
Cortez, Hernando, 32
Course of action. *See* Actions
Culture, 30, 72-74, 99

Dangers, *3,* 34, *37,* 50, 71, 82-83
*See also* Hazards to exploring decision making; Rationalization; *and under particular demapatterns and demalinkages*
Debate within responsive pattern, 30-31
Decider, complete, 98-99
Decisions, 7-9, *13*, 27, 105
  complexity of, 29, 41-45, 66, 80
  consciousness of, *9, 25, 37,* 78, 86-87, 98
  to go mad, 86
  number of, 77, 78
  *See also* Decision making
*Decision, Order and Time in Human Affairs* (Shackle), 136
*Decision Analysis: Introductory Lectures on Choices under Uncertainty* (Raiffa), 136
Decision making, 2, 7, 15, 100
  approaches to, *2-3*, 10, 77-81
  *See also* Decisions; Hazards to exploring decision making; MacNeal's dematheory; *all* Dema *listings*
Decision-making *subject. See* Dema *subject*
Definitions, 17, 112-17
  *See also* Terms
Dema, 11-12
Demaformulas, 29, 31, 34, 40, 43
  absolute, 29, 43
  action-comparative, 29, 43
  goal-directed, 34, 43
  originative, 40, 43
  responsive, 31, 43
  scorecard, 43
Demalinkages, 16-17, *25, 47, 61,* 72, 99, 108-110
  basic, 16-17, 49-55, 99, 108-109
  quiz on, 55
  verbal clues and levers of, 130-31
  *See also* Allocative demalinkage; Recursive demalinkage; Transformative demalinkage
  interpersonal, 16-17, 63-74, 109-110
  quiz on, 72
  verbal clues and levers of, 131-33
  *See also* Mutual demalinkage; Organizational demalinkages; Propositional demalinkage; Reciprocal demalinkage; Demasystems
Demalogical explication, *119*, 120-22
Demalogical implication, 120-34
  *See also* Verbal clues and levers
Demalogical structures. *See* Demastructures
Demalogical thesaurus, 125-34

# Index

Demalogics, 11-12, 16-17, 77-81, 105, 111, 120-26
  acquisition of, *25-26*, 30, 98, 100, 124
  competence in, 98, 100, 124
  dangers in, *3*, 34, *37*, 50, 71, 82-83
  number of, 77-78
  and psychology, *75, 89*, 93, *104*
  quiz on, 81
  selection of (*see* Selecting demalogics)
  and social science, *76, 90, 104*, 136
  uses of, 7-9, *37*, 71, 78, 83, 94, 96, *104*
  verbal clues and levers of, 92-95, 98
  *See also* Demalinkages; Demapatterns; Demasystems; Comparative demalogics
*Demalogics 2.0* (MacNeal), 7-10, *26, 61*, 136
Demamaps, 7-12, 78-81, 92, 106-109
  of demalinkages, 50, 65, 66, 109
  of demapatterns, 27-33, 39-45, 79, 106-108
  of subdecisional events, 20-23
  mentioned, 2, 98-99, *118*
Demapattern freedom, 66, 78, 98
Demapatterns, 25, 46, *47*, 56, *75*, 106-108
  basic, 16-17, 27-36, 39-43, 106-107
    verbal clues and levers of, 49, 127-28
    *See also* Absolute pattern; Action-comparative pattern; Goal-directed pattern; Originative pattern; Responsive pattern
  compound, 16-17, 42-46, 79, 107-108
    verbal clues and levers of, 122, 129-30
    *See also* Scorecard pattern
Demaprayer, 21
Demaspecies, 66-67
Demastructures, *13*, 16-18, *75, 90, 104*, 105-111
  level 1. *See* Subdecisional events
  level 2. *See* Demapatterns, basic
  level 3. *See* Demapatterns, compound
  level 4. *See* Demalinkages, basic
  level 5. *See* Demalinkages, interpersonal
  level 6. *See* Demasystems
  level 7. *See* Comparative demalogics
Demasystems, 16-17, 51, 72-74, 110
  and other demalogics, 51, 72-73, 110
  verbal clues and levers of, 121, 132-33
Dematheory. *See* MacNeal's dematheory

Demaunits, 63, 67, 69-70
Demawalk, 79-81
Diesing, Paul, 136
DiMaggio, Joe, 122
*Direct Decision Therapy* (Greenwald), 87, 136
Direct preference, 39
  *See also* Preference
Disclamation, 101
Disengaged value judgments, 97

Economics, 74, 100, *104*, 136
  *See also* Allocative demalinkage
Education, 2, 99, *118-19*, 126
Elementalism, *2, 13-14*, 114
  examples of, *13, 14*, 19-20, *37*, 46
Enfounding demalinkage, 67, 110, 132
Enstaffing demalinkage, 67, 110, 132
Error, 4, 12, 56-58, 81-86, 133
  regarding demalogics, 28, 33, 36, 54, 97
  mentioned, *75*
*Et cetera* (journal), 125
*Ethics* (journal), 136
Euclid, *104*
Evolution, *25-26*
Examples, choice of, *37*
Exton, William, *14*

Fautsko, Timothy F., 136
Federal Aviation Administration (FAA), 31
Fitting actions. *See* Responsive pattern
"The flaw" (MacNeal), 136
Forced response, 32
Forecasts, *14*, 31-32, 84-85, 100, 114
Formulas. *See* Demaformulas
"Foundations of a theory of decision making" (MacNeal), *1*, 136
Freud, Sigmund, 10
Fried, Yitzhak, *75n*
Functionarial demalinkage, 67-68, 72-74, 110, *119*, 132-33
Functionaries, 56-58, 67-73

General semantics, *1-2*, 20, *37, 61*, 99, 101, 135
  *See also* Korzybski, Alfred; *Science and Sanity*
*General Semantics Bulletin*, *14*

Gilbert, Sir William S., 34
Globe, 7, 40
Glossary, 112-17
Goals, 9, 23, 33-36, 94, 115
  dangers in, 34-35, 85, 98
  and demalinkages, 50, 74
  and non-goal-directed patterns, 27, 39-45, 57, *76, 90*
  *See also* Goal-directed pattern
Goal-directed pattern, 9, 33-34, 43, 64, 107
  dangers in, 34, 82-83, 85
  and demalinkages, *47*, 49-50, 68, 71, 79, 83
  and other demapatterns, 39-40, 44, 56-58, 71, 79, 122
  is overplayed, 33-36, 126, 136
  and psychology, *89, 104*
  uses of, 34, *47*, 57, 71, *89*, 96, 100
  verbal clues and levers of, 36, 39-41, 91, 94, 98, 121-22, 128
  mentioned, *75, 118*, 135
Goode's map projection, 6, 10n, *18*
Green Bay Packers, 34
Greenwald, Harold, 87, 136

Hart, H. L. A., 73, 136
Hazards to exploring decision making
  language, 11-12, *13-14*, 36, 120
  nearsightedness, 12, *37*
  rationalization, 10-11, *14, 25-26*, 27, 33, *37*, 49-50, 86
  *See also* Consciousness, of decisions
History. *See* MacNeal's dematheory, history of
*Hitchhiker's Guide to the Galaxy*, 51
Hitler, Adolf, 97
Holmes, Sherlock, 95
Housman, A. E., 52
*Human Relations* (journal), *75n*
Hypocrisy, 58-59
  *See also* Rationalization

*Initial Instruction in How People Make Decisions* (MacNeal), 136
Inoperative proposals, 97
International Society for General Semantics, *1*, 101
Interpersonal linkages. *See* Demalinkages, interpersonal
Isabella, Queen, 4, 7, 100
Jerome, Saint, 34
Johnson, Wendell, *1*
Jorgensen, James D., 136
*Journal of Economic Literature*, 136

Kilroy, 16, *76*, 77
Kinsey report, 81
Kluckhohn, Clyde, 136
Korzybski, Alfred
  on decision making, 100, 135
  on language, *1-2, 13-14*, 100
  on maps, 5
  as a pioneer, *1-2*, 101
  on structure, 5, *13-14*, 20, *37*, 100
  on terminology, 93
  on time-binding, *61*
  *See also* General semantics

Lambert's map projection, 6, 18
Language, 11, *14, 26, 61*, 124
  translation of, 122, 126
  *See also* Definitions; Demalogical explication; Demalogical implication; General semantics; Linguistics; Meanings; Terms; Thesaurus; Verbal clues and levers
*Language* [journal], 93
Law, 71, 73-74, *75*
  mentioned, *2*, 51, 98, 110, 133, 136
Lee, Irving, *1*
Levels. *See* Demastructures
Likes and dislikes, 23, 127
  in absolute pattern, 27-28
  dangers of, 41, 85, 98
  and non-absolute patterns, 28, 39, 43, 45
  mentioned, 22, 44, 68, 108, 124
  *See also* Absolute pattern
Linguistics, *75*, 93
  *See also* Language Linnaeus, Carolus, *13*
Lombardi, Vince, 34

MacNeal, Edward
  on "issues" as examples, *37*
  on learning demalogics, *118-19*
  on patterns vs. linkages, *47*
  on uses and dangers, *37*

# Index

*See also* MacNeal's dematheory
MacNeal's dematheory, *1-2, 13-14, 25-26, 37,* 89
  bearing of, on social science, 76, *89-90, 104*
  "complexity" of, *13-14, 118-19*
  history of, *1, 26, 47, 118,* 125, 135
  relation of, to general semantics, *1-2, 61,* 101, 135
  sources of, *1, 26,* 135-36
*Manhood of Humanity* (Korzybski), *61*
Maps, 4-9, 11, 15, 18-19, 85
  projections of, 4-7, 10n, 18
  *See also* Demamaps
Marvell, Andrew, 52
Master Atlas
  omissions from, 99
  sources of, *2, 26,* 135-36
*Matthew* 26.41, 122
Meanings, *13,* 124
  *See also* Language
Mendeleev, Dmitry I., *13*
Mercator's map projection, 5
*Merriam-Webster New Collegiate Dictionary,* 123
Miller, David W., 33
Mindlessness, *75*
  *See also* Unconscious decisions
"Mindlessness of organizational behaviors" (Ashforth and Fried), *75n*
Mollweide's map projection, 5
Montezuma, 32
Morison, Samuel Eliot, 4
Morris, Charles, *1*
Multidemalogical terms, 123-24, 133
Multiform pattern, 43n, 107, 129
  *See also* Demapatterns, compound
Multiordinality of decision, *13,* 17
Mutual demalinkage, 64-66, 109, 115
  quiz on, 72
  verbal clues and levers of, 91, 121, 123-24, 131-32

*Nichomachean Ethics* (Aristotle), 33
Niebuhr, Reinhold, 20-21
"No choice," 32
Non-elementalism
  examples, *14*

  of originative pattern, *37, 38*
  *See also* Continuity; Elementalism

Omnidemalogical term, 123-24
Organizational demalinkages, *47, 61,* 66-72, 109-110
  dangers in, *47,* 71, *75,* 83
  and other demalogics, 68, 71, *75*
  quiz on, 72
  verbal clues and levers of, 91, 121, 123-24, 132
  mentioned, 77, 98, *118-19*
  *See also* Business
Organizations, 66-69, 71
Originative pattern, 9, *37,* 39-41, 43, 64, 107
  dangers in, 42, 91
  and demalinkages, *47,* 49-50, 74n
  and other demapatterns, 56-58
  uses of, *37,* 41, 84-85, 96
  verbal clues and levers of, 39-41, 57, 91, 94, 121, 128
  mentioned, 75, *118,* 126, 135

Parsons, Talcott, 136
Patterns. *See* Demapatterns
Payouts, 53
*Personality and Decision Processes* (Brim *et al.*), 36
Poems, 21, 41-42, 52
Polo, Marco, 21
Postman, Neil, 101
Preference, 23, 28, 39, 43-45, 98, 114-15
  *See also* Action-comparative pattern; Originative pattern
Primary rules, 73
Problem-solving, 36, 56-57, 94
  *See also* Goal-directed pattern
Projections. *See* maps
Proposals, 63-64, 97, 105, 116, 131
  examples of, 30, 58, 121-22
  forms of, 63, 116, 131
  operative and inoperative, 97
  in responsive pattern, 30, 58, 64
  structures of, 105
  in time-binding, *61*
  mentioned, 66
  *See also* Propositional demalinkage

Propositional demalinkage, 63-64, 109
  and other demalogics, 64, 71
  quiz on, 72
  and time-binding, *61*, *75*
  uses of, 63-64, 71, 83
  verbal clues and levers of, 63, 121-22, 131
  mentioned, *119*
  *See also* Proposals
Pros and cons, 7-8, 43, 64, 129
  *See also* Scorecard pattern
Psychology, *75*, 86-87, *89-90*, 93, *104*
Psychosis, 86-87

Quantitative demalinkage, 108, 130
  and demapatterns, 108, 136
  mentioned, 16, 77, 99
Questions, demalogically loaded, 91
*QUID (Quantified Intrapersonal Decision-Making*, 136
Quiz on
  alternaquences and situations, 22
  basic demalinkages, 55
  basic and interpersonal demalinkages, 72
  demapatterns, 46
  conflicting demapatterns, 56-58
  selecting demalogics (demawalk), 81
  transformative demalinkage, 57
  verbal clues and levers, 56, 95

Raiffa, Howard, 136
Rapoport, Anatol, 101
Rationalization, *3, 25*, 86
  benefits of, 50
  dangers of, 10, *14, 25-26*, 27, 33, *37*
  *See also* Transformative demalinkage
  *Reason in Society* (Diesing), 136
Reasons, 23, 42, 98, 116
  in demalinkages, 65, 66, 86
  in demapatterns, 16-17, 27, 29, 33, 43-46, 47
Reciprocal demalinkage, 65-66, 109
  and other demalogics, 65-66, 71
  quiz on, 72
  verbal clues and levers of, 91, 121, 132
  mentioned, *75*
Recursive demalinkage, 50-51, 54
  and demapatterns, 50-51

  in demasystems, 72-74
  and language, *61*
  and law, *75*
  and other demalinkages, 51, *61*, 72-74, 110
  quiz on, 72
  verbal clues and levers of, 91, 130
  mentioned, *119*
Recursive functionarial responsiveness (RFR), 72-74, 110, 114, 116
  *See also* Demasystems
Rejections, 86
"Relation of habitual thought and behavior to language" (Whorf), 40
Responsibility, 32, 71, 91-92, 133
Responsive pattern, 8, 29-32, 43, 64, 107
  and bureaucracy, *47*, 71, *75*
  dangers in, 32, 71, *75*, 82, 85
  and demalinkages, 49, 51, 66, 71, 73, *75*, 79
  and other demapatterns, 44-45, 56-58, 71, 79, 83
  and psychology, *75, 89*
  is unappreciated, 29, 126
  uses of, 31, 57, 71, *75*, 83, 96, 100
  verbal clues and levers of, 39, 91-93, 94, 98, 121-22, 127-28
  mentioned, *118*, 135
  *See also* Demasystems; Rules
RFR. *See* Recursive functionarial responsiveness
Risks, 7, 31-32
  *See also* Forecasts; Hazards to exploring decision making
Robinson, David N., *89*
Roget, Peter Mark, 125
*Roget's International Thesaurus*, 125-26
Roles. *See* Functionaries
Rules, 23, 72-74, 116
  dangers in, 32, 82, 98
  and demalinkages, *25*, 34, 50-51, 63, 66, 68, 72-74, 91
  and demapatterns, *25*, 27, 33, 41-43, 45
  in demasystems, 72-74
  primary and secondary, 73
  mentioned, *61*, 79, 99, 121
  *See also* Responsive pattern

# Index

Sapir, Edward, 93
Scheduling, 53-54
"Science and linguistics" (Whorf), 93
*Science and Sanity*, *1-2*, 5, *13-14*, 20
   quotation from, *61*, 93, 100, 101
Scorecard pattern, 7-8, *37*, 42-46, 64, 108
   dangers in, 44-45, 83, 85
   and demalinkages, 49
   and other demapatterns, 56-58
   uses of, 45, 57, 96, 136
   verbal clues and levers, 91, 94, 121-22, 129-30
   mentioned, *75*
Script theory, *75*
Secondary rules, 73
Second-order organizational demalinkage, 68, 110, 132
Selecting demalogics, *3*, 12, 77-81, 94, 98, 100
   demawalk, 79-81
   for interpersonal use, 49-50, 56-59, 86, 91-92, 94
   quiz on, 46, 55, 81
   *See also* Demalogics, uses of; Proposals
Self-actualization, *89*
Self-reflexiveness, 2, 5, *13*, 50
   *See also* Recursive demalinkage
Semantics, 125
   *See also* General semantics; Language
"Semantics and decision making" (MacNeal), *1*, 41, 136
*Semantics of Air Passenger Transportation* (MacNeal), *14*
Sequential pattern, 43n, 108, 130
Serenity prayer, 21
Shackle, G. L. S., 136
Shils, Edward A., 136
*Shropshire Lad* (Housman), 52
Side effects, 34-35, 42, 91, 117
Simon, Herbert, 135
Situation, 8, 16, 21-23, 98, 106-109
   and demalinkages, 66
   and demapatterns, 27, 29-32, 39, 41, 44
   quiz on, 22
   *See also* Responsive pattern
Social science
   and demalogics, *76*, *89-90*, *104*, 136
   and rationalization, 10
   *See also* Economics; Law; Linguistics; Psychology
Starr, Martin K., 33
"Status of linguistics as a science" (Sapir), 93
Steinberg, Douglas J., *89*
Stimulus-response, *89*
Structural levels, *13*, 15-16
   *See also* Demastructures
*Structure of Human Decisions* (Miller and Starr), 33
Subdecisional events, 16-23, 105-106
   verbal clues and levers of, 126-27
   *See also* Actions; Alternaquences; Consequences; Situation
"Successive levels of material structure" (Alexander), *13*
Synopsis of chapter(s)
   1, *14*
   1-2, *26*
   1-3, *38*
   1-4, *48*
   1-5, *62*
   1-6, *76*
   1-7, *90*
*Systems of Modern Psychology* (Robinson), *89*

Tastes, 27-28, 44, 127
   not in originative demalogic, 41-42
   in selection walk, 79
   *See also* Absolute demapattern; Likes and dislikes
*Technology Review*, 93
Terms, *1-2*, 11, *13-14*, 93, 112-17
   "action," 12, 19-23, 106
   "alternaquence," 19
   "consequences," 12, 19-20
   "decision," *13*
   "error," 82
   within demalogics, 126-34
   glossary, 112-17
   multidemalogical, 123-24
   omnidemalogical, 82, 123-24
   "originative," 136
   for proposals, 63
   "situation," 21
   "values," 2, 12, 23, 136
   *See also* Language; Verbal clues and levers

Textual explication, *119*, 120-22
  *See also* Demalogical implication
Thesaurus, 125-34
Thucydides, 120
Time, *1, 13-14, 61*, 101, *119*
  in allocative demalinkage, 51-54
  and availability of action, 20, 21, 51-54, 97-98
  in originative pattern, 39-40, 85
  and responsibility, 91-92
  in responsive pattern, 29-31, 94, 120-21, 127
  in sequential pattern, 117
  *See also* Forecasts
Time-binding, *61*
*To His Coy Mistress* (Marvell), 52
*Toward a General Theory of Action* (Parson & Shils, eds), 136
*Tractatus Logico-Philosophicus* (Wittgenstein), 136
Transformative demalinkage, *25*, 49-50, 54, 108
  dangers in, 10, *25*, 50
  and other demalogics, *25*, 34, 41, 49-50, 71, 91
  quiz on, 57, 72
  and rationalization, 10, *25*, 41-42
  uses of, 49-50, 57-59, 71, *75*, 96
  verbal clues and levers of, 91, 94, 98, 130
  *See also* Rationalization
Translation, 122, 126
"Turning points" (poem), 41-42

Uncertainty, 20, 33, 84-85
Unconscious decisions, 9, *25*, 86
  *See also* Consciousness
Uniform pattern, 43n, 107, 129
  *See also* Demapatterns, compound
United Nations, 68
University of Chicago, *1*
Uses of demalogics. *See* Demalogics, uses of

Value judgments, 2, 23, 97, 117
Values, *1-2*, 12, 23, 99, 117, 136
  elementalistic, 2, *48*, 114
  in scorecard pattern, 43-46

"Values and value-orientations" (Kluckhohn), 136
Verbal clues and levers, 36, 40-41, 92-95, 98, 120-34
  of proposals, 63
  quizzes on, 56, 95
  *See also under particular demalogics*
Verbal split. *See* Elementalism

"What I think Korzybski thought--and what I think about it" (Rapoport), 101
"When does consciousness of abstracting matter the most?" (MacNeal), *37*, 136
Whorf, Benjamin Lee, 40, 93
Wittgenstein, Ludwig, 136